Lost &
Found

Lost & Found

a memoir

Kathryn Schulz

RANDOM HOUSE
NEW YORK

Published in the United States by Random House,
an imprint and division of Penguin Random House LLC, New York.

RANDOM HOUSE and the HOUSE colophon are
registered trademarks of Penguin Random House LLC.

Parts of this book originally appeared in *The New Yorker* in an essay titled
"When Things Go Missing," published on February 5, 2017.

Grateful acknowledgment is made to the following for permission to reprint
previously published material:

Farrar, Straus & Giroux: Four lines from "Close, close all night" from *Edgar Allan
Poe & The Juke-Box* by Elizabeth Bishop, edited and annotated by Alice Quinn,
copyright © 2006 by Alice Helen Methfessel; four lines from "One Art" from *Poems*
by Elizabeth Bishop, copyright © 2011 by The Alice H. Methfessel Trust. Publisher's
Note and compilation copyright © 2011 by Farrar, Straus & Giroux. All poetry
reprinted by permission of Farrar, Straus & Giroux. All rights reserved.

Farrar, Straus & Giroux and Faber and Faber Limited: Excerpt from "The Trees"
from *The Complete Poems of Philip Larkin* by Philip Larkin, edited
by Archie Burnett, copyright © 2012 by the Estate of Philip Larkin. Digital rights
are controlled by Faber and Faber Limited. Reprinted by permission
of Farrar, Straus & Giroux and Faber and Faber Limited. All rights reserved.

HarperCollins Publishers: A haiku of Bashō's from *The Essential Haiku:
Versions of Bashō, Buson & Issa* edited and with an Introduction by
Robert Hass, introduction and selection copyright © 1994 by Robert Hass.
Reprinted by permission of HarperCollins Publishers.

Henry Holt and Company: "Devotion" from *The Poetry of Robert Frost* by
Robert Frost, edited by Edward Connery Lathem, copyright © 1928, 1969
by Henry Holt and Company. Copyright © 1956 by Robert Frost.
Reprinted by permission of Henry Holt and Company. All rights reserved.

Library of Congress Cataloging-in-Publication Data
Names: Schulz, Kathryn, author.
Title: Lost & found : a memoir / Kathryn Schulz.
Other titles: Lost and found
Description: First edition. | New York : Random House, [2022]
Identifiers: LCCN 2021001420 (print) | LCCN 2021001421 (ebook) | ISBN
9780525512462 (hardcover ; alk. paper) | ISBN 9780525512479 (ebook)
Subjects: LCSH: Schulz, Kathryn. | Fathers and daughters—United States—
Biography. | Lesbians—United States—Biography. | Families—United States—
Biography.
Classification: LCC HQ755.86 .S38 2022 (print) | LCC HQ755.86 (ebook) | DDC
306.850973—dc23
LC record available at lccn.loc.gov/2021001420
LC ebook record available at lccn.loc.gov/2021001421
International Edition ISBN 9780593446225

Printed in the United States of America on acid-free paper

randomhousebooks.com

2 4 6 8 9 7 5 3 1

First Edition

Book design by Diane Hobbing

*For my father, whom I lost,
and for C., who found me*

Nothing includes everything, or dominates over everything. The word "and" trails along after every sentence.

—*William James, "A Pluralistic Universe"*

CONTENTS

I.
Lost

I have always disliked euphemisms for dying. "Passed away," "gone home," "no longer with us," "departed": although language like this is well-intentioned, it has never brought me any solace. In the name of tact, it turns away from death's shocking bluntness; in the name of comfort, it chooses the safe and familiar over the beautiful or evocative. To me, all this feels evasive, like a verbal averting of the eyes. But death is so impossible to avoid—that is the basic, bedrock fact of it—that trying to talk around it seems misguided. As the poet Robert Lowell wrote, "Why not say what happened?"

Yet there is one exception to this preference of mine. "I lost my father": he had barely been dead ten days when I first heard myself use that expression. I was home again by then, after the long unmoored weeks by his side in the hospital, after the death, after the memorial service, thrust back into a life that looked exactly as it had before I left, orderly and daylit, its mundane obligations rendered exhausting by grief. My phone was lodged between my shoulder and my chin. While my father had been in a cardiac unit and then an intensive care unit and then in hospice care, dying, I had received a series of automated messages from the magazine where I work, informing me that I would be locked out of my email if I did not change my password. These arrived with clockwork regularity, reminding me that my access would expire in ten days, in nine days, in eight days, in seven days. It is remarkable how the ordinary and the existential are always stuck together, like the pages in a book so time-worn that the print has transferred from one to the other. I did not fix the password problem. I did lose the access and, with it, any means to solve the problem on my own. And so, after my father died, I found myself on the phone with a customer service representative, explaining, although it was absolutely unnecessary to do so, why I had neglected to address the issue in a timely fashion.

I lost my father last week. Perhaps because I was still in those early, distorted days of mourning, when so much of the familiar world feels alien and inaccessible, I was struck, as I had never been before, by the strangeness of the phrase. Obviously my father hadn't wandered away from me like a toddler at a picnic, or vanished like an important document in a messy office. And yet, unlike other oblique ways of talking about death, this one did not seem cagey or empty. It seemed plain, plaintive, and lonely, like grief itself. From the first time I said it, that day on the phone, it felt like something I could use, as one uses a shovel or a bell-pull: cold and ringing, containing within it both something desperate and something resigned, accurate to the confusion and desolation of bereavement.

Later, when I looked it up, I learned that there was a reason "lost" felt so apt to me. I had always assumed that, if we were referring to the dead, we were using the word figuratively—that it had been appropriated by those in mourning and contorted far beyond its original meaning. But that turns out not to be true. The verb "to lose" has its taproot sunk in sorrow; it is related to the "lorn" in "forlorn." It comes from an Old English word meaning to perish, which comes from an even older word meaning to separate or cut apart. The modern sense of misplacing an object only appeared later, in the thirteenth century; a hundred years after that, "to lose" acquired the meaning of failing to win. In the sixteenth century we began to lose our minds; in the seventeenth century, our hearts. The circle of what we can lose, in other words, began with our own lives and each other and has been steadily expanding ever since.

This is how loss felt to me after my father died: like a force that constantly increased its reach, gradually encroaching on more and more terrain. Eventually I found myself keeping a list of all the other things I had lost over time as well, chiefly because they kept coming back to mind. A childhood toy, a childhood friend, a beloved cat who went outside one day and never returned, the letter my grandmother wrote me when I graduated from college, a threadbare but perfect blue plaid shirt, a journal I'd kept for the better part of five years: on and on it went, a kind of anti-collection, a melancholy catalogue of everything of mine that had ever gone missing.

Any list like this—and all of us have one—quickly reveals the strangeness of the category of loss: how enormous and awkward it is, how little else its contents have in common. I was surprised to realize, when I first began thinking about it, that some kinds of loss are actually positive. We can lose our self-consciousness and our fear, and although it is frightening to be lost in the wilderness, it is wonderful to be lost in thought or a book or a conversation. But those are happy outliers in an otherwise difficult region of human experience; for the most part, our losses lie closer in spirit to the death of my father, in that they diminish our lives. We can lose our credit card, our driver's license, the receipt for the item we need to return; we can lose our good name, our life savings, our job; we can lose faith and lose hope and lose custody of our children. Much of the experience of heartbreak falls into this category, since an unwanted breakup or divorce entails the loss not only of someone we love but also the familiar texture of our days and a cherished vision of the future. So, too, with serious illness and injury, which can lead to the loss of everything from basic physical abilities to fundamental parts of our identity. Some of our most intimate experiences are here, as when an expectant mother loses a pregnancy, alongside some of the most public and shattering events of history: war, famine, terrorism, natural disaster, pandemic—all the awful collective tragedies that establish the far extremity of what it is possible to lose.

This is the essential, avaricious nature of loss: it encompasses, without distinction, the trivial and the consequential, the abstract and the concrete, the merely misplaced and the permanently gone. We often ignore its true scope if we can, but for a while after my father died, I could not stop seeing the world as it really is, marked everywhere by the evidence of past losses and the imminence of future ones. This was not because his death was a tragedy. My father died peacefully, at seventy-four, tended throughout his final weeks by those he loved most. It was because his death was *not* a tragedy; what shocked me was that something so sad could be the normal, necessary way of things. In its aftermath, each individual life seemed to contain too much heartbreak for its fleeting duration. History, which I had always loved even in its silences and mysteries, suddenly seemed like little more than a record of loss on an epic scale, especially where it could offer no record at all. The world itself seemed ephemeral, glaciers and species and ecosystems vanishing, the pace of change as swift as in a time-lapse, as if those of us alive today had been permitted to see it from the harrowing perspective of eternity. Everything felt fragile, everything felt vulnerable; the idea of loss pressed in all around me, like a hidden order to existence that emerged only in the presence of grief.

This relentless disappearance is not the whole story of our lives; it is not even the whole story of this book. But in the weeks and months after my father died, I could not stop thinking about it, partly because it seemed important to understand what all of these losses had to do with each other and partly because it seemed important to understand what all of them had to do with me. A lost wallet, a lost treasure, a lost father, a lost species: as different as these were, they and every other missing thing suddenly seemed fundamental to the problem of how to live—seemed, in being gone, to have something urgent to say about being here.

MY FATHER HAD something urgent to say about almost everything. The world was endlessly interesting to him, and he delighted in discussing any part of it: the novels of Edith Wharton, the nature of cosmic background radiation, the infield fly rule in baseball, the lingering impact of the 1947 Taft-Hartley Act, the discovery of a new species of nocturnal monkey in South America, the merits of apple cobblers versus apple crisps. My older sister and I were welcomed into these conversations from more or less the time we could talk, but additional participants were never hard for him to find. When it came to other people, my father possessed the gravitational pull of a mid-sized planet. He had a booming voice, a heavy accent, a formidable mind, a rabbinical beard, a Santa Claus belly, and the gestural range of the Vitruvian Man; collectively, the effect was part Socrates, part Tevye.

The accent was a consequence of my father's rootless childhood, which also left him fluent in six languages—in rough order of acquisition, Yiddish, Polish, Hebrew, German, French, and English. To my subsequent regret, he raised my sister and me to speak only the last of these, but he made up for it by the lavishness with which he did so. It was my mother, a French teacher and wonderfully lucid grammarian, who taught me how to work with language: how to pronounce "epitome," when to use the subjunctive, how to distinguish "who" from "whom." But it was my father who taught me how to play with it. Thanks to his polyglot background, he had a relativist's relationship to the rules of grammar and usage; he did not defy them, exactly, but he loved to bend a phrase right up to the breaking point before letting it spring back into place, reverberating wildly. I have never met anyone else who could generate such surprising sentences on the fly, nor anyone else who derived as much fun just from speaking. When I expressed disbelief at the "epitome" correction, he furnished, in an instant, an unforgettable mnemonic device: "It rhymes with 'you gotta be kidding me.'"

It is a cliché about writers that we come from unhappy families—that we turn to language and stories to either escape from or give voice to our misery. This was not my experience. I came from a happy family, where language and stories were a shared and omnipresent pleasure. One of my earliest memories consists of my father materializing in the doorway of the room where I was playing—all of five foot six, but seeming to my startled eyes like a benevolent and thrilling giant—holding a Norton anthology of poetry in one hand and waving the other aloft like Merlin while reciting "Kubla Khan." I have a similarly vivid recollection of him entertaining my sister and me a few years later with the prologue to *The Canterbury Tales,* declaimed out loud in rousing Middle English. My mother gave up early on the project of convincing him not to rile us up at bedtime; it was his job to read aloud to us each night, and he accomplished the task with extravagant gestures, dramatic voices, much thumping of the knees on which we were perched, and an exhilarating disregard for the text on the page. On the best nights, he ditched the books entirely and regaled us with a series of homegrown stories about the adventures of Yana and Egbert, two danger-prone siblings from, of all places, Rotterdam—a location he chose because he knew the sound of it would make his little daughters laugh.

Although my father was far better read than I will ever be, literature was his passion, not his vocation. By training, he was a lawyer and an occasional law school instructor; both jobs suited him, but especially the latter, since he embodied to perfection the figure of the absentminded professor. He had a prodigious memory, a panoptic curiosity, and an ability, in the face of problems of all kinds, to distinguish what was irrelevant from what mattered as swiftly as a coin machine separates pennies from quarters. What he did not have, nine times out of ten, was his wallet, or any notion of where he had parked his car. In keeping with the stereotype, these deficits always seemed like a consequence of his extraordinary intellect, as if he could somehow channel to better purposes all the mental energy the rest of us expend on not misplacing our belongings. Whether or not they were related, however, these curiously contradictory qualities—

a remarkable perceptiveness about the world and a remarkable obliviousness to it—were two of the defining features of his character.

Among the many things my father was prone to losing was himself. I grew up in the suburbs of Cleveland, and several times a year, my family would drive to Pittsburgh to visit my maternal grandmother. In theory, that journey took just over two hours, but before I was out of my single digits, I knew to be alarmed when my father settled into the driver's seat and announced that we were taking a shortcut. Children experience all car trips as eternal, but those really were drastically longer than they needed to be, because my father, constitutionally genial yet also constitutionally stubborn, could not be persuaded that he didn't know where he was going. I can recall one version of this experience in which we headed west rather than east for a solid half hour, and another where we managed to take the same incorrect highway exit three consecutive times. My mother could have put an end to all of this, because she was a much better navigator, but she was also a loving and pragmatic spouse, and so she intervened only gently on these misadventures unless time was of the essence—which, in my father's opinion, it seldom was, because, in addition to having no sense of direction, he had no sense of time.

At any rate, as you might infer from his inability to locate Pittsburgh, my father was truly hopeless when it came to keeping track of smaller things. His pet name for my mother was Maggie (derived from Margot, her given name and the one used by everyone else), and one of the phrases I heard most often throughout my childhood was "Maggie, have you seen my": checkbook, eyeglasses, grocery list, jury summons, coffee mug, winter coat, other sock, baseball tickets—several times a day, some new object gone astray completed that question. Without fail, the second half of this call-and-response was "It's right here, Isaac." Luckily for my father, my mother generally had seen the missing item and could remember where it was, and failing that, she had the temperament to track it down. In keeping with her superior navigational abilities, my mother was patient, methodical, and highly attuned to her surroundings.

I inherited these traits; my sister, who is now a cognitive scientist at MIT, did not. In this respect, the four of us, otherwise a fairly similar bunch, were always notably divided. On the spectrum of obsessively orderly to sublimely unconcerned with the everyday physical world, my father and sister were—actually, they were nowhere; they were somewhere near the Ohio-Pennsylvania border, still looking for the spectrum itself. My mother and I, meanwhile, were busy organizing it by color and size. I have a vivid memory of watching my mom try to adjust an ever-so-slightly askew picture frame—in the Cleveland Museum of Art. My father, by contrast, once spent an entire vacation wearing two different shoes, because he had packed no others and discovered that the ones on his feet didn't match only when asked to remove them by airport security. My sister's best air-travel trick involved losing her own laptop, borrowing her partner's, and then accidentally leaving it at a United Airlines departure gate one week after 9/11, thereby almost shutting down the Oakland airport. She also excels, as my father did before her, at the more understated art of repetitive losing: cellphone, annually; wallet, quarterly; keys, monthly. On the sole occasion in my adult life when I myself lost a wallet,

I made the mistake of trying to complain to her about it and she laughed at me. "Call me," she said, "when they know your name at the DMV."

As the torchbearer for my maternal lineage, at least in this respect, I have always been naturally inclined to do slightly unnatural things, like organizing the pantry by food group or putting every one of sixty-four crayons back in the exact same slot it was assigned at the factory. That kind of fastidiousness, not to say obsessiveness, can come in handy for keeping track of possessions; one reason I seldom lose things is that I get a little itchy if I haven't returned them to their designated household location. Well into adulthood, this tendency toward order, combined with two immediate family members who made me look good by comparison, led me to believe that I was not one of those people who lose things.

But pride goeth before a forty-minute search for that piece of paper you were just holding, and the fact is, we are all one of those people who lose things. Like being mortal, being slightly scatterbrained is part of the human condition: we have been losing stuff so routinely for so long that the laws laid down in Leviticus include a stipulation against lying about finding someone else's lost property. Modernity has only made this problem worse. In the developed world, even people of modest means now live in conditions of historically unfathomable abundance, and every extra item we own is an extra item we can lose. Technology, too, has exacerbated the situation, rendering us chronically distracted while simultaneously supplying us with enormous numbers of additional losable things. That has been true for a while now—the remote control is still one of the most frequently misplaced objects in American households—but as our gadgets grow ever smaller, the odds of losing them grow ever larger. It is difficult to lose a desktop computer, easier to lose a laptop, a snap to lose a cellphone, and nearly impossible *not* to lose a flash drive. Then there is the issue of passwords, which are to computers what socks are to washing machines.

Phone chargers, umbrellas, earrings, scarves, passports, headphones, musical instruments, Christmas ornaments, the permission slip for your daughter's field trip, the can of paint you scrupulously set aside three years ago for the touch-up job you knew you'd someday need: the range and quantity of things we lose is staggering. Someone like my father might lose ten times as much stuff as someone like my mother, but on average, according to data from surveys and insurance companies, each of us misplaces roughly nine objects per day—which means that by the time we turn sixty, we will have lost nearly two hundred thousand things. Not all of those losses are irreversible, of course, but one of them always is: the time you wasted searching for all the rest. Across your life span, you'll spend roughly six solid months looking for missing objects. Here in the United States, that translates to, collectively, some fifty-four million hours spent searching *per day*. Then there's the associated loss of money: domestically, around thirty billion dollars a year on lost cellphones alone.

There are two prevailing explanations for why we lose all this stuff—one scientific, the other psychoanalytic, both unsatisfying. According to the scientific account, losing things represents a failure, sometimes of recollection and sometimes of attention: either we can't retrieve a memory of where we put our missing object or we didn't encode one in the first place. According to the psychoanalytic account, the opposite is true: losing things represents a success, a clever sabotage of our rational mind by our subliminal desires. In *The Psychopathology of Everyday Life,* Freud describes "the unconscious dexterity with which an object is mislaid on account of hidden but powerful motives," including "the low estimation in which the lost object is held, or of a secret antipathy towards it or towards the person that it came from." A colleague of his put the matter more plainly: "We never lose what we value highly."

As explanations go, the scientific one is persuasive but un-interesting. Although it makes clear why we are more likely to misplace things when we're exhausted or distracted, it sheds no light on how it actually feels to lose something, and it provides only the most abstract and impractical notion of how not to do so. (Focus! And while you're at it, adjust your genes or your circumstances to improve your memory.) The psychoanalytic account, by contrast, is intriguing, en-tertaining, and theoretically useful (Freud pointed out how swiftly certain people of his acquaintance found something again "once the motive for its being mislaid had expired") but, in the majority of cases, unconvincing. The most chari-table thing to be said about it is that it wildly overestimates our species: absent subconscious motives, apparently, we would never lose anything at all.

That is patently false—but, like many psychological claims, impossible to actually falsify. Maybe my father lost his baseball tickets because he was disappointed in Cleve-land's chronically lousy performance. Maybe my sister loses her wallet so often due to a deep-seated discomfort with capitalism. Freud would stand by such propositions, and no doubt some losses really are occasioned by unconscious emotion, or at least can be plausibly explained that way after the fact. But experience tells us that such cases are exceptional. The better explanation, most of the time, is simply that life is complicated and minds are limited. We lose things because we are flawed, because we are human, because we have things to lose.

MY FATHER'S OWN ability to lose things was inversely correlated to how much those losses troubled him. He misplaced stuff all the time, but he generally greeted each new loss with equanimity, as if his possessions were merely borrowed and their rightful owner had decided to reclaim them. I suppose that a different person with his talent for losing things might have developed a compensatory ability to find them. But my father had developed, instead, a compensatory ability to be cheerfully resigned to their disappearance.

That is an admirable attitude—close, I think, to what the poet Elizabeth Bishop meant by "the art of losing." The line comes from "One Art," a poem I have always loved, and one of the most famous reckonings with loss in all of verse. In it, Bishop suggests that minor losses like keys and watches can help prepare us for more serious ones—in her case, two cities, a continent, and the lover to whom the poem is addressed. At first, this claim seems preposterous. It is one thing to lose a wedding ring and something else entirely to lose a wife, and we are rightly reluctant to equate them. Bishop knows this, of course, and in the poem's final lines, when she contemplates the loss of her lover, the art of losing suddenly shifts from something that "isn't hard to master" to something that's "not *too* hard to master." The italics are mine, but the concession is hers, and it undermines her overall assertion so much that it is easy to read the poem as ironic—as acknowledging, in the end, that the loss of a loved one is incommensurable with any other.

Yet it is also possible to hear something else in those final lines: a reluctant admission that all of us must somehow learn to live with even our most devastating losses. In that reading, Bishop's poem is perfectly sincere. It suggests that if we cultivate equilibrium around everyday losses, we might someday be able to muster a similar serenity when we lose more important things. That claim isn't preposterous at all. Entire spiritual traditions are built on the idea of nonattachment, on the belief that we can learn to face even our gravest losses with acceptance, equilibrium, and grace.

Like many religious ideals, however, this one is largely aspirational for the majority of people. In practice, most of us experience even trivial losses as exasperating. That isn't just because they always cost us time and sometimes cost us money. We also pay a psychological price for them: any loss, no matter how minor, can cause a small crisis in our relationship with ourselves, with other people, or with the world. Those crises aren't triggered by the problem of location—of where to find our missing object. They are triggered by the problem of causation: of who or what made it disappear.

Most of the time, the answer is that we did. In the micro-drama of loss, we are nearly always both villain and victim. This is unfortunate for our egos, plus various other parts of ourselves. If you know that you were the last person to handle your child's beloved stuffed orange orangutan but you have no idea what you did with it, you will rightly blame your memory, sometimes worrying not only about its immediate lapse but also about its overall reliability. Yet it is scarcely more comforting to know exactly how you lost something—as when you can't find your credit card, then realize that you left it at a restaurant over the weekend. At best, such losses leave us feeling irresponsible. At worst, if we have lost something valuable, they can leave us feeling genuinely anguished. For hours or days or sometimes even years, they focus our attention exactly where it failed to focus in the first place: on the moment, among the least forgiving in all of life, when it was still possible to avert what was to come.

In short, losing things routinely makes us feel lousy about ourselves. As a result, we often decline to take responsibility for it, choosing instead to look for someone else to blame. This is how a problem with an object becomes a problem with a person: you swear you left the bill sitting on the table for your husband to mail; your husband swears with equal vehemence that it was never there; soon enough, you have also both lost your tempers. When there are no other convenient suspects around, you may even find yourself accusing your missing object of engineering its own disappearance, alone or in conjunction with various occult forces. That sounds absurd, but almost all of us have leveled allegations like this at some point, because almost all of us have experienced losses that seem to verge on impossible: the sweater we were just wearing that has somehow vanished in a six-hundred-square-foot apartment; the letter we distinctly remember bringing in from the mailbox that has dematerialized by the time we go looking for it in the kitchen. Given enough time spent searching for lost items like these, even the least superstitious among us will start positing various highly improbable culprits: goblins, aliens, wormholes, ether.

It makes sense that we invoke malign or mysterious powers when something goes missing, because it can feel, in such moments, as if the world is not obeying its customary rules. No matter how many times it happens, we experience loss as surprising and perplexing—as a rupture in the way things are meant to work. It feels inconceivable that you can't find that sweater or that letter, just as it feels inconceivable that your wife of twenty years came home from work one day and asked for a divorce or that your healthy young uncle died last night in his sleep. In the face of losses both large and small, one of our characteristic reactions is a powerful feeling of disbelief.

That feeling is extremely seductive but also extremely misleading. Consider, for instance, a particularly tragic loss from recent years: that of Malaysia Airlines Flight 370, which, together with the two hundred and thirty-nine people on board, disappeared in March of 2014 with disturbing thoroughness—no distress call, no fire, no explosion, no claims of responsibility, no credible witnesses, and, for more than a year, not a single scrap of debris. At first, the plane was thought to have gone down somewhere in the South China Sea, partway along its intended route from Kuala Lumpur to Beijing. Only many months later, after much wild speculation—including that it had been shot down by the Chinese government or hijacked by Russians and diverted to a cosmodrome in Kazakhstan—did investigators conclude that it had most likely headed south until, finally out of fuel, it crashed somewhere in the remoter reaches of the Indian Ocean.

Like many people who were both gripped and horrified by this story, I found myself repeatedly wondering, while all this speculation was going on, how it was possible, in our ultra-connected, GPS-monitored world, to lose something as large and as closely tracked as a commercial airplane. That incredulity was, in a narrow sense, entirely merited. In the context of aviation, what happened to Malaysia Airlines Flight 370 was wildly anomalous: over the course of the previous fifty years and almost a billion flights, only one other commercial aircraft, a much smaller one, had simply disappeared. Yet in the context of the larger world, what happened to the airplane wasn't anomalous at all. Experience and history both teach us that there is nothing on earth that cannot be lost—no matter its value, no matter its size, no matter how vigilantly we try to keep track of it. And a clear-eyed look at the world itself teaches us this, too. We struggle to imagine losing an airplane because it seems enormous when we watch it pass low overhead on the highway, moments before touching down. But that is the wrong scale of resolution at which to consider the problem. A Boeing 777 may seem large compared to us, but you could comfortably fit one hundred and eighty billion of them on the bottom of the Indian Ocean.

In the end, this may be why certain losses are so shocking: not because they defy reality but because they reveal it. One of the many ways that loss instructs us is by correcting our sense of scale, showing us the world as it really is: so enormous, complex, and mysterious that there is nothing too large to be lost—and, conversely, no place too small for something to get lost there. A missing wedding ring can turn the modest geography of an urban park into the Rocky Mountains. Losing sight of your child during a hike can turn a peaceful stretch of stream and forest into a formidable wilderness. Like awe and grief, to which it is closely related, loss has the power to instantly resize us against our surroundings; we are never smaller and the world never larger than when something important goes missing.

It is this harsh corrective to our sense of being central, competent, and powerful that makes even trivial losses so difficult to accept. To lose something is a profoundly humbling act. It forces us to confront the limits of our mind: the fact that we left our wallet at the restaurant; the fact that we can't remember where we left our wallet at all. It forces us to confront the limits of our will: the fact that we are powerless to protect the things we love from time and change and chance. Above all, it forces us to confront the limits of existence: the fact that, sooner or later, it is in the nature of almost everything to vanish or perish. Over and over, loss calls on us to reckon with this universal impermanence—with the baffling, maddening, heartbreaking fact that something that was just here can be, all of a sudden, just gone.

I HAVE SOMETIMES THOUGHT that my father's lifelong habit of misplacing things was the comic-opera version of the tragic series of losses that shaped his childhood. Although you wouldn't have known it from his later years, which were characterized by abundance, or from his personality, which was characterized by ebullience, my father was born into a family, a culture, and a moment in history defined to an extraordinary degree by loss: loss of knowledge and identity, loss of money and resources and options, loss of homes and homelands and people.

In its broad outlines, the story is familiar, because it belongs to one of the most sweeping and horrific episodes of loss in modern history. My father's mother, the youngest of eleven children, grew up on a shtetl outside Lodz, in central Poland—by the late 1930s, one of the most dangerous places to be Jewish on an entire continent increasingly dangerous to Jews. Because her family was too large and too poor for all of them to escape the coming war together, her parents arranged, by a private calculus unimaginable to me, to send their youngest child off to safety. That is how, when she was still a teenager, my paternal grandmother found herself more than twenty-five hundred miles from the only world she had ever known, living in Tel Aviv, which at the time was still part of Palestine, and married to a Polish Jew considerably her senior.

Not long after, my father was born, and not long after that, as a toddler, he was sent away to a kibbutz, to be raised for some years among strangers. While he was there, two formative losses befell his family. First, his biological father died and his mother remarried—a fact my father only learned more than two decades later, on his wedding night. Second, every member of my grandmother's family that had remained behind in Poland was sent to Auschwitz. Her parents perished there, as did nine of her ten siblings. On January 27, 1945, when the camp was liberated, only her oldest sister, my great-aunt Edzia, walked out alive. I don't know when or how this information reached my grandmother, or how she learned all the rest of the news that must have made its way to Tel Aviv name by name. Almost a quarter of a million Jews had lived in Lodz when she left it; barely more than nine thousand survived the war. When my father returned from the kibbutz a few years later, it was to a family reconfigured twice over, once by death and remarriage, once by the emotional and practical conditions created by this wholesale annihilation—almost an entire lineage gone, grandparents and aunts and uncles and cousins and friends and neighbors all slaughtered, a mother bereft beyond description.

Tel Aviv had been a relatively good place to weather the war, but it was not a good place to face its aftermath. With the future of the Middle East in flux, the city was increasingly dangerous; one morning, a friend of my father's was killed by a stray bullet while playing in the street outside their apartment. As conditions deteriorated, the family, never well-off in the first place, struggled to scrape by. My grandfather was a plumber, but work was scarce, and by then he and my grandmother had two other sons to feed as well. In February of 1948, three months before the United Nations carved an entire new country out of Palestine, my grandparents decided that they were done trying to raise their children there. And so, in one of the more unlikely trajectories in the history of modern Judaism, they packed up their meager possessions, left what was about to become the state of Israel, and moved—to Germany.

It was, unsurprisingly, not their first choice. After the war, my grandparents had applied for visas to America, but there were few of those available and eleven million other refugees in need of a place to call home. Between the physical peril and their dwindling finances, they could not afford to wait indefinitely; and so, when my grandfather heard a rumor that it was possible to make a decent living on the black market in postwar Germany, he took notice. He had no religious devotion, no Zionist impulses, and no scruples whatsoever about bending the rule of law in the former Third Reich; his allegiance was to his family, and to survival. If a living could be made in Germany, then never mind that the whole tide of history was just then surging in the other direction: to Germany they would go.

It was a terrible journey. To get to a port with a ship bound for Europe, the family, together with an uncle who had decided to join them, had to travel by car from Tel Aviv to Haifa—a distance of just sixty miles, but hazardous ones, in those days. By then, civil war had broken out in Palestine between Arab nationalists and Jewish Zionists, and blockades, bombings, ambushes, land mines, and sniper fire were all increasingly common. Midway along the route, the uncle was shot in the front seat. My father, seven years old, sat in the back and watched while he gradually died. In later life, my father's normal volubleness always veered around this tragedy; either from lingering trauma or out of an instinct to protect his children, he recounted it without elaboration, as bare biographical fact. I know only that his family, lacking any other option, continued on to Haifa, where they left the body, then sailed to Genoa and made their way to Germany.

They stayed for four years, settling in a little town in the Black Forest. My father played in the woods and learned to swim in the river and befriended an enormous sheepdog named Fix. At school, he mastered German, the language in which he first read *Kidnapped* and *Treasure Island,* and was sent by his teachers to sit alone in the hallway for an hour each afternoon during religious instruction. On evenings and weekends, his father set him down in the sidecar of his motorcycle and drove him all over the country, an adorable bright-eyed decoy atop a stash of Leica cameras and illicit American cigarettes. It was a pleasant existence, but also a precarious one, and the older my father got, the more he understood that his family was in trouble. The money they made was stashed under floorboards and rolled inside curtain rods; there was talk, not meant for the children to hear, of near misses and confrontations, of whether and where and how much the authorities had begun cracking down on smugglers. Over time, it became obvious to my father that his fate hinged on the question of whether the visas or the police would arrive first.

By luck, it was the visas: in 1952, my grandparents packed up their children, made their way to Bremen, and set sail for the United States. My father began throwing up while land was still in sight, and even if the ocean hadn't been pitching beneath him, it is easy to imagine why he would have felt unstable. By then, he had lost, like Elizabeth Bishop, two cities and a continent, along with almost all of what should have been his family. He had lived on a commune and in a war zone, in the Middle East and in Europe, in the burning forge that made Israel and the cooling embers of the Third Reich. He was not yet twelve years old. He spent almost the entire voyage in his steerage-class berth, at sea in both senses, miserably ill. Only when his parents told him that they were drawing near to port did he struggle up to the deck to look at the view. That is my father's first memory of his life in America: coming unsteadily into the sunlight and wind and seeing, there in the narrow waters off of Manhattan, the Statue of Liberty.

MY FATHER COULD not have known, that day in New York Harbor, that the most difficult parts of his life were already behind him. But I do think he had an intuition that, in putting so much distance between himself and his past, he was incurring losses of a different kind—the kind that, for immigrants and refugees, are often the price of making a home in a new place. His native language, a private creole of Yiddish and Polish, evaporated with the dispersal and death of his immediate family, all of whom he outlived; his native land he saw just once more in his lifetime, fifty years after leaving it behind. One of his final conversations, with a Lebanese friend and fellow refugee, concerned Edward Said's definition of exile, as a loss so profound that it darkens all future achievements. This my father—a man who found as much as he lost, including enduring happiness—could not entirely endorse. But he knew intimately the cost of assimilation, one of life's stealthiest forms of loss, as well as the abiding yearning for an unrecoverable home.

Still, it is a testament to the life my father made for himself in America that the upheavals of his childhood seemed like distant history by the time I came along. Upon arriving in this country, his family had settled in Detroit, where he was sent to attend Americanization classes in the leaky basement of the local public high school. His real Americanization, though, took place on his own time, partly on the street corner where a local electronics shop kept the television in its window turned to cowboy shows all day long, but mostly in the nearby alleyways, the de facto playgrounds of inner-city Detroit. Well into his seventies, my father could wax lyrical about those alleys, which he loved—for their trash cans, which were excellent for finding interesting things that other people had thrown away; for their high, narrow walls, perfect for handball; but above all because they were a place to go when his parents were fighting in the family's cramped apartment. As those arguments intensified in quantity, volume, and viciousness, my father, by then thirteen, started spending less and less time at home.

Some of what he found on his own was trouble. He smoked his first cigarette that year, sneaking one of his father's Pall Malls in the bathroom and graduating within weeks to a pack a day. (He switched to a pipe when my mother got pregnant and smoked it for years. I loved everything about it—the smell, the quiet *pock-pock-pock,* the long, fuzzy cleaners I could wrap around my wrist like bracelets—but eventually my sister and I wised up to the dangers and successfully lobbied him to stop.) He also made a best friend, a kid named Lee Larson, the wisecracking, whip-smart son of a local bar owner, and together the two of them drifted toward low-grade delinquency. Even decades later, when his life had taken a turn for the upstanding, my father could not quite keep the fondness from his voice while describing how he and Lee, together with a few other friends, once spent months stealing one traffic cone at a time from all over Detroit, then sat on a hill above a main artery at rush hour, watching the commuters slow to a crawl while diverting around the giant nonexistent roadworks they had made.

For the most part, though, pranks like this were incidental, side effects of the thrill of first encountering the world on his own terms. He collected enough cereal-box tops to earn a ticket to a Tigers game, took himself one sunny day to Briggs Stadium, and promptly fell in love with baseball— which, in some way that tracked all the way back to his thirteen-year-old self, really did feel to him forever afterward like freedom. He went to the public library, which, being free in the other sense, was an excellent place to escape his home life; soon he was spending almost every day after school there, relishing the quiet and reading until closing time. He even went, in a manner of speaking, to church. After the local radio station kept airing the same advertisement again and again, urging listeners to come hear the preacher's daughter singing with the gospel choir any Sunday morning, he and Lee finally heeded the summons and took a bus to New Bethel Baptist Church, one blond kid and one bespectacled Jew at the back of the chapel, getting their first earful of Aretha Franklin.

Throughout all of this, my father had excelled in school; in 1958, five years after arriving in America, he graduated as his class valedictorian. But very few of his fellow students were going to college, his parents knew nothing about American higher education, and by the time someone suggested that he apply to the University of Michigan, the only open spots were in the school of engineering. He matriculated, hated it, and failed out after one semester. The next year he talked himself back in, this time to the college of liberal arts, which went better until he accidentally set his dorm room on fire and got expelled a second time. When he finally did get his bachelor's degree, it was the long way, via a stint as a soda jerk in Manhattan, another as a used-clothing salesman in Illinois, a summons from his local draft board, and an exceptionally lucky last-minute reroute to Korea instead of Vietnam. Just before he deployed, he met my mother; upon his return, he married her, finally finished college, went to law school, then settled in Cleveland to start a family and a career. In a kinder world—one where my father's early years had been less desperate, his fear of financial instability less acute, his sense of the options available to him less constrained—I suspect that he would have chosen a very different line of work: as a professor like my sister, maybe, or as a writer, like me. But if he ever felt that loss, he didn't show it. He loved the law and he loved his family, and he was proud to be able to give his daughters a far safer and happier childhood than he himself had enjoyed.

Most parents would do anything to provide that kind of life for their children. That is why my grandparents traveled through war zones and risked arrest and twice in four years left behind everything they knew to board a ship bound for a foreign country, and it is why my great-grandparents sent their youngest daughter off to a new home a world away, fully knowing that in all likelihood they would never see her again. I am alive today because both generations succeeded. Still, I know that those successes, like all such successes, were fragile and contingent. Experience teaches us nothing if not that all the things parents seek for their children—safety, stability, happiness, opportunity—are neither equitably distributed nor permanent conditions. Even if we are fortunate enough to have them in the first place, they, too, are susceptible to loss, liable to be swept away at any moment by forces far stronger than we are—stronger, sometimes, than whole peoples and nations. War, famine, genocide, pandemic, earthquakes, tsunamis, hurricanes, mass shootings, mass starvation, mass financial ruination: devastation in all its many forms routinely sweeps through entire communities, sometimes through entire countries, and—as during my father's earliest years, and again in our own times— occasionally and terribly throughout most of the world.

These are the kinds of losses that make all others seem insignificant by comparison. Indeed, a heightened sense of what is trivial versus what actually matters is one of the few things that supposedly emerges from a disaster not merely intact but enhanced, as if catastrophe left moral and emotional clarity in its wake. After witnessing so much distressing loss, the theory goes, we will understand what is really important in life and stop worrying about all the rest. This idea inverts the logic of Elizabeth Bishop: our largest losses, it suggests, can help us cope with our smaller ones, by putting them in perspective.

At first glance, this is an appealing notion. Yet on closer consideration, it is no easier to accept than Bishop's claim that minor losses prepare us to accept major ones. It is true that many people learn to count their blessings after exposure to serious loss, and also learn not to dwell on their minor frustrations; my father, for one, had an enduring sense of what to care about and what to let go, and for the most part he did not, as they say, sweat the small stuff. But who can know how much of that was personality and how much was circumstance? Certainly my grandmother did not emerge from the horrors of World War II with a renewed appreciation for everything that matters most in life: she emerged from it *robbed* of almost everything that matters most in life, including the person she might have become under better circumstances. By the time I knew her, she was volatile and unhappy, her inner life armored and inscrutable. It is possible, of course, that some of that was personality, too. Still, given the overall effects of trauma, it is peculiar, and borderline cruel, to imagine that it ultimately operates on us for the better.

Nor do we live our own lives as if this were the case. Granted, most of us do what we can to salvage meaning from our most difficult losses, and some people argue, either out of genuine conviction or an attempt at consolation, that suffering builds character. Still, if parents truly believed that loss had improved their lives and made them better people, they would not work so hard to keep their children from experiencing it—and yet, generation after generation, most of them do. The problem is that there is a limit to how much such efforts can ever succeed. Sufficient financial resources may ward off certain kinds of hardship, and sufficient love and support may leave us better equipped to face life's inevitable difficulties. But to be prepared is not to be spared. Our parents cannot protect us from experiencing loss forever, because, in the end, barring a worse tragedy, we will lose them.

WHAT BECOMES OF the things we lose and never recover? Nothing consistent, of course. The lost glove rots away unnoticed in a corner of the garden; the handbag languishes for months at a train station before being donated to a secondhand store; the scrap of paper with the phone number on it melts into the slush of a February sidewalk; the wreckage of the missing airplane lies twenty thousand feet below the surface of the ocean, visited from time to time by creatures no human eyes have ever seen.

It is a curious and long-standing habit of the human mind to try to gather all these lost objects together in one place. We don't just invent fantastical culprits to explain why our possessions have disappeared; we invent fantastical destinations to explain where they can be found. I first came across one of these in childhood, stumbling on it because it was the obscure cousin of a far more famous fictional location. In

L. Frank Baum's *Dot and Tot of Merryland,* two small children clamber into a boat and are carried by the current to a magical kingdom across a desert from the Land of Oz. That kingdom consists of seven valleys, and although most of them are delightful to explore—full of babies and clowns and candy and kittens—the final one is silent and strange, empty of people and strewn with miscellaneous objects from riverbank to horizon: hats, handkerchiefs, buttons, coats, pocketbooks, shoes, dolls, toys, rings. When Dot looks around in confusion, the Queen of Merryland explains: "It is the Valley of Lost Things."

Although it often goes by other names, the Valley of Lost Things has haunted our collective imagination for centuries. Over five hundred years ago, Ludovico Ariosto, one of the greatest writers of the Italian Renaissance, summoned a version of it in *Orlando Furioso,* an epic poem that tells the story of the most famous knight to fight under Charlemagne in the Crusades. In it, Orlando loses the woman he loves to a rival and, as a consequence, also loses his mind. To help him, another knight consults with a prophet, who declares that they must travel to the moon: "A place wherein is wonderfully stored / Whatever on our earth below we lose." Together they go there (via chariot) and discover not lost hats and shoes and handkerchiefs but lost fortunes, lost fame, lost loves, lost reputations, lost kingdoms, and lost minds— these latter each in its own stoppered vial, one of them labeled "ORLANDO'S WIT."

Plenty of other versions of the Valley of Lost Things have cropped up over the years, in every context from autobiography to science fiction. In *Mary Poppins and the House Next Door,* P. L. Travers reprised the idea that everything that vanishes from earth winds up on the moon, although this time the lost items are everyday household objects. (The most recent *Mary Poppins* film gave this idea a wistful, existential edge: the young protagonists, mourning their dead mother, are led to believe that she dwells on the far side of the moon, "the place where lost things go.") Other iterations feature other settings. Charles Fort, an early-twentieth-century skeptic and investigator of unexplained natural phenomena, once posited the existence of a "Super-Sargasso Sea"—located not in our earthly oceans but somewhere above them or in a parallel dimension—into which all missing things disppear, including dodos, moas, pterodactyls, and every other lost species.

Part of the enduring appeal of this imaginary destination is that it comports with our real-life experience of losing things: when we can't find something, it is easy to feel that it has gone somewhere unfindable. But there is also something pleasing about the idea that our missing belongings, unable to find their rightful owners, should at least find each other, gathering together like souls in the bardo or distant relatives at a family reunion. The things we lose are distinguished by their lack of any known location; how clever, how obviously gratifying, to grant them one. And how thrilling to imagine walking around in such a place—harrowed by the worst of the losses, humbled by the heaps of almost identical stuff, delighted when we discover something that once belonged to us, awed by the sheer range of what goes missing.

This may be the most alluring aspect of the Valley of Lost Things: it renders the strangeness of the category of loss visible, like emptying the contents of a jumbled box onto the floor. In my mind, it is a dark, pen-and-ink place, comic and mournful as an Edward Gorey drawing: empty clothing drifting dolefully about, umbrellas piled in heaps like dormant bats, a Tasmanian tiger slinking off with Hemingway's lost novel in its mouth, glaciers shrinking glumly down into their puddles, Amelia Earhart's Lockheed Electra atilt upon the ground, the air around it filled with the ghosts of night-time ideas not written down and gone by morning. It is this taxonomically outrageous population, shoes to souls to pterodactyls, that makes the idea of such a place so mesmerizing. Its contents have a unity and meaning based only on the single common quality of being lost, a kind of vast nationality, like "American."

Still, for all its charm, the Valley of Lost Things is, at its core, a melancholy place. The things we love are banished to it, and we ourselves are banished from it: the one feature every version of it has in common is that, under normal circumstances, it is inaccessible to humans. Only a prophet or Mary Poppins can take you to the repository of lost things on the moon, and Tot understands immediately why he and Dot are allowed to venture into the otherwise unpopulated Valley of Lost Things: "'Cause we're lost, too." In that sense, the two of them are less closely related to Dorothy and the Tin Man than to Orpheus and Dante, who, unlike most mere mortals, were temporarily permitted to slip into the netherworld. Likewise, the valley and the netherworld are themselves closely related. As with the lost objects we love, so too with the lost people we love: we grant them an afterlife, in the bittersweet knowledge that, at least in this world, we will never again get to see them.

MY FATHER'S DEATH was not sudden. For nearly a decade beforehand, his health had been poor, almost impressively so. In addition to suffering from many of the usual complaints of contemporary aging (high blood pressure, high cholesterol, kidney disease, congestive heart failure), he had endured illnesses unusual for any age and era: viral meningitis, West Nile encephalitis, an autoimmune disorder whose identity eluded the best doctors at the Cleveland Clinic. From there the list spread outward in all directions of physiology and severity. He had fallen in a hotel lobby and torn a shoulder beyond recovery and had obliterated a patellar tendon by missing a step on a friend's back patio one Fourth of July. His breathing was often labored despite no evident respiratory problem; an errant nerve in his neck intermittently triggered excruciating pain and sent him into temporary near paralysis. He had terrible dental issues, like the impoverished child he had once been, and terrible gout, like the lordly old man he became.

For all this, my father was largely spared one of the most common of late-in-life losses, that of mental capacity. There was, however, one exception to this—a strange and frightening spell that lasted two or three years but, mercifully for us although unusually for the condition, turned out to be reversible. This occurred toward the beginning of his more infirm years, when his autoimmune disorder had first emerged, provoking a series of terrifying health crises and causing an entire team of doctors—cardiologists, nephrologists, immunologists, oncologists, infectious disease specialists—to set about trying to determine what was wrong with him. In the absence of a diagnosis, they resorted to treating his symptoms, which, as often happens in such circumstances, involved an ever longer list of medications: drugs to manage the immediate problems, drugs to manage the resulting side effects, drugs to manage the side effects of the drugs meant to manage the side effects. That all this might create its own crisis is obvious in retrospect, but it wasn't at the time, partly because we were too worried about the underlying disease to focus on anything else and partly because that secondary crisis was slow to make itself known. Eight or nine months went by before my mother and sister and I began to worry, at first quietly and then openly, about what was happening to my father's mind.

The earliest changes were gradual, the earliest lapses infrequent and indistinct. My father began sleeping more hours at night and nodding off during the day, including during family gatherings, which normally amplified his usual exuberance. In conversation he would sometimes strike off in inexplicable directions, leaving the rest of us to try to tether the strange things he said to relevance, to see our way from there to somewhere lucid. Of all my family members, I was the most guilty of this—of maintaining an insistent, petrified optimism even in the face of moments of obvious incoherence.

Eventually, though, those moments became too regular and too alarming to keep waving off as normal aging. Even my father's famously hopeless sense of direction could not offer any cover on the evening when he got off the commuter train—at a stop three blocks from his house, from which he had gone back and forth to work for thirty years—and could not remember how to get home. In other ways, too, he began to lose track of himself in space and time. In conversation he grew confused about what year it was, about whether he was in Cleveland or Boston or Italy or Israel. I remember very clearly the completely incomprehensible phone call that finally forced me to confront the truth: the most remarkable mind I had ever encountered was failing—

was, in many crucial ways, already gone. If you have ever lived through the cognitive decline of someone you love, you have had a night like the one that followed for me. That was the first time I ever grieved my father.

It was my sister, the scientist, who eventually put two and two together. One day, after a particularly alarming episode of confusion landed my father in the hospital, she called his doctors and told them to start pulling him off of every drug that wasn't actively saving his life. No matter how long I live, I can't imagine I will ever witness another transformation as astonishing as the one that followed. The night after he was released from the hospital—my sister and I had by then flown home to be with him—my father stayed up with us until well past two in the morning, talking about the origins of Italian anarchism, the role of the commerce clause in constitutional law, the family relations in *Bleak House,* and the rival positions on the nature of consciousness espoused by various philosophers. The next day he woke up early and cheery and, together with the rest of us, took his four-year-old granddaughter out sledding.

There is an old saying—of what origin I cannot say—about how to make a man happy. First you take away his donkey; then you give it back. I don't know anything about donkeys, beyond the fact that the comparison would make my father laugh. But I can affirm that there is nothing in this world more wonderful than the feeling of being reunited with something precious that you thought was permanently lost. It had been upward of two years since I had seen my father even half so much like himself, a year since I had accepted that he would never again be the person I had always known. And then, almost overnight, he was back.

I learned an enormous amount from this experience,

including something new about the relationship between small losses and serious ones. Most of the time, losing everyday objects is not indicative of any kind of underlying illness, but real mental decline does often manifest partly as an uptick in lost things. Dementia patients are prone to misplacing their belongings, and people with early-stage Alzheimer's often can't find something because they have put it in an unlikely location: the eyeglasses end up in the oven, the dentures in the coffee can. I knew all this, and so when my father began showing signs of cognitive decline, I fell into the habit of scrutinizing his every loss for indications that it might portend a larger one. The misplaced wallet, previously both characteristic and comical, became a potential source of alarm; the word he went looking for and couldn't find sent me scanning, like an anxious parent at the edge of the ocean, the wide gray expanse between ordinary and ominous. I know now that countless people live with this habit and with this fear, either for themselves or for someone they love, and I understand why. The brain is the deepest and most mysterious of all the Valleys of Lost Things, and it is heartbreaking what can go missing there: the town you live in, the name of your wife, what to do with a hairbrush, the reason a caretaker is in your apartment, who you are, how to find your way home.

Of all of the losses my father suffered in his final years, this was the most terrible—but only for my mother and sister and me. My father himself was largely oblivious to his situation, and therefore largely untroubled by it; I have seen him, while in his right mind, more frustrated by failing to remember the name of the third baseman for the 1956 Detroit Tigers than he was by his whole long iatrogenic decline. As a result, even though he was manifestly a creature of his intellect, he was ultimately far more affected by all the others losses that beset him in old age—and, unlike the cognitive problems, none of these ever reversed themselves. On the contrary, they compounded, growing both individually worse and collectively more numerous with each passing year.

In that sense, although some of my father's ailments were rare, his overall experience was perfectly common. Most of us alive today will survive into old age, and although that is a welcome development, the price of experiencing more life is sometimes experiencing less of it, too. So many losses routinely precede the final one now: loss of memory, mobility, autonomy, physical strength, intellectual aptitude, a longtime home, the kind of identity derived from vocation, whole habits of being, and perhaps above all a certain forward-tilting sense of self—the feeling that we are still becoming, that there are things left in this world we may yet do. It is possible to live a long life and experience very few of these changes, and it is possible to experience them all and find in them, or alongside them, meaning and gratitude. But for most of us, they will provoke, at one point or another, the usual gamut of emotions inspired by loss, from mild irritation to genuine grief.

I don't mean to suggest that my father was unhappy at the end of his life; he was not. He had my mother, whom he adored, and who—increasingly out of necessity but always also out of love—seldom left his side. He had my sister and her family and me, and he got a huge amount of delight from all of us. He had a monthly book club that he relished, and a daily book club with himself. He had two cats he pretended to hate, and a group of people he kibitzed with at the pool where he and my mother went regularly to swim, and enormous concentric circles of friends and colleagues and acquaintances all over town.

And yet if "to lose" originally meant to separate, my father was increasingly separated from the man he once had been. He no longer practiced law, although he had a passionate work ethic and had always cherished his colleagues and his job. He no longer traveled, although he loved to see the world, because too many injuries and difficulties befell him when he tried. He no longer drove, although all his life he had maintained a kind of happy teenage pleasure in doing so. He had never been an athlete but he had always been vigorous; now he could barely walk to the end of the block. On top of all of this there was the pain, and pain's dreadful handmaiden, shame. Even now, I turn away slightly from the memory of my father, sweating visibly in a restaurant from a sudden increase in the agony caused by that nerve in his neck, needing to make it to the bathroom quickly but being unable to do so.

It was terribly upsetting to bear witness to all of these changes. I hated to see my father diminished and suffering, and I worried, not wrongly, that what I was witnessing was the beginning of the end. But only belatedly did I start to reckon with the incompatibility between my sympathy and my fear: with the fact that the time would come when only death would release my father from pain. That is often true at the end of life, and so one way to think about the many losses associated with illness and aging is that they help us make our peace with the ultimate one. You hear people make this case all the time, especially retroactively. "At least he's no longer suffering," we say after someone has died. "At least she's out of pain."

It is true that this can be a consolation. With life as with so many things, more is not necessarily better; all of us can imagine countless conditions, inner as well as outer, that may make an earlier death better than a later one. No one, I think, would wish a longer life on an eighty-year-old Jewish man about to die peacefully in Poland in 1938. And very few of us would wish longevity on someone whose bodily suffering has become so unbearable that they no longer regard their life as worth living. But even if we could somehow maintain perfect health in perpetuity, we should not necessarily want to prolong life forever. It is very tempting, as the French scholar Philippe Ariès once wrote about death, to "annex it to the territory of the devil." But many very wise thinkers regard a timely death as fundamentally good, and make far bolder claims for its merits than mere relief from pain. The devout may view death as an important transformation or a welcome homecoming, while the secular may see it as both morally and psychologically necessary, because a life that went on forever would be devoid of meaning.

I have always thought that this was true; our time here, it seems to me, is made precious by virtue of being scarce. But, as I have discovered again and again, what one thinks and how one feels can part ways radically in the face of grief. I am glad, unequivocally, that my father is out of pain, but that is as far as I am able to go. Way down in the core of selfhood where emotion begins, it is impossible for me to offer death any more gratitude than that, or to pretend I don't wish that my father—my brilliant, funny, adoring, endearing father—were still alive, and would be alive forever. "The best argument I know for an immortal life," William James once wrote, "was the existence of a man who deserved one."

LIKE DEATH MORE generally, my father's own was somehow both predictable and shocking. It happened one September, just before the autumn equinox, that time of year when the axis of the world tilts definitively toward darkness. By then it was so evident that my father was in the autumn of his own life that I suppose I should have been more prepared for him to die. But as the ER visits had piled up over the years, I had gradually curbed my initial feelings of panic and dread—partly because no one can live in a state of crisis forever but also because, by and large, he himself bore his infirmity with insouciance. ("Biopsy Thursday," he once wrote me about a problem with his carotid artery. "Have no idea when the autopsy will be and may not be informed of it.") More to the point, against considerable odds, he just kept on being alive. Intellectually, I knew that no one could bear up under such a serious disease burden forever. Yet the sheer number of times my father had courted death and then recovered had served, perversely, to make him seem indomitable.

As a result, I was not overly alarmed when my mother called me one day to say that my father had been hospitalized with a bout of atrial fibrillation. Nor was I surprised, when my partner and I got to town that evening, to learn that his heart rhythm had already stabilized. The doctors were keeping him in the hospital chiefly for observation, they told us, and also because his white blood cell count was mysteriously high. When my father narrated the chain of events to us—he had gone to a routine cardiology appointment, only to be shunted straight to the ICU—he was jovial and accurate and eminently himself. He apologized for in-

conveniencing us, confessed that he was nonetheless delighted to see us, and attempted to thwart the cardiac-friendly
dinner prescribed by the hospital by sending us out to find a
decent bowl of chili. Maybe tomorrow, we said, figuring
that he would be discharged by then; but the next day, although he remained in good spirits, something was amiss.
When we arrived in the morning, we found him extremely
garrulous, not in his usual effusive way but slightly manic,
slightly off: a consequence, the doctors said, of toxins building up in his bloodstream from temporary loss of kidney
function. If it didn't resolve on its own, they planned to give
him a round or two of dialysis to clear it.

That was on a Wednesday. Over the next two days, the
garrulousness declined toward incoherence; then, on Saturday, my father ceased to talk. This was as mysterious to his
medical team as it was distressing to the rest of us. In addition to cherishing conversation, my father had always made
sense of the world through speech; all his life, he had talked
his way into, out of, and through everything, including illness. Over the years of medical emergencies, I had seen him
racked and raving with fever. I had seen him in a dozen
different kinds of pain. I had seen him hallucinating—
sometimes while fully aware of it, describing his visions and
discussing the mysterious nature of cognition. I had seen
him cast about in a mind temporarily compromised by illness and catch only strange, dark, hadal creatures, unknown
and fearsome to the rest of us. In all that time, under all
those varied conditions, I had never known him to lack for
words. But now, for five days, he held his silence. On the
sixth, he lurched back into sound, but not into himself;
there followed an awful night of struggle and agitation.
After that, aside from a few scattered words, some baf-

fling, some seemingly lucid—"Hi!"; "Machu Picchu"; "I'm dying"—my father never spoke again.

Even so, for a while longer, he endured—I mean his himness, his Isaac-ness, that inexplicable, assertive bit of self in each of us. A week after he had ceased to speak, having ignored every request made of him by a constant stream of medical professionals ("Mr. Schulz, can you wiggle your toes?" "Mr. Schulz, can you squeeze my hand?"), my father chose to respond to one final command: Mr. Schulz, we learned to our amusement, could still stick out his tongue. But his sweetest voluntary movement, which he retained almost to the end, was the ability to kiss my mother. Whenever she leaned in close to brush his lips, he puckered up and returned the same brief, adoring gesture I had seen all my days. In front of my sister and me, at least, it was my parents' hello and goodbye, their "Sweet dreams" and "I'm only teasing," their "I'm sorry" and "You're beautiful" and "I love you"—the basic punctuation mark of their common language, the sign and seal of fifty years of happiness.

One night, while that essence still persisted, we gathered around my father and filled his silence with all the things we did not want to leave unsaid. I had always regarded my family as close, so it was startling to realize how much closer we could get, how near we drew around his waning flame. The room we were in was a cube of white, lit up like the aisle of a grocery store, yet in my memory, that night is as dark and vibrant as a Rembrandt painting. We talked only of love; there was nothing else to say. We told him how grateful we were, how happy he had made us, how fully and honorably he had lived out his days. My father, mute but seemingly alert, looked from one face to the next as we spoke, his brown eyes shining with tears. I had always hated to see him cry, and seldom did, but for once, I was grateful. It gave me hope that, for what may have been the last time in his life, and perhaps the most important, he understood. If nothing else, I knew that everywhere he looked that evening, he found himself where he had always been with his family: the center of the circle, the source and subject of our abiding love.

All of this makes dying sound meaningful and sweet— and it is true that, if you are lucky, there is a seam of sweetness and meaning to be found within it, a vein of silver in a dark cave a thousand feet underground. Still, the cave is a cave. We had, by then, spent two vertiginous, elongated, atemporal weeks in the hospital. At no point during that time did we have a diagnosis, still less a prognosis. At every point, we were besieged with new possibilities, new tests, new doctors, new hopes, new fears. Every night we arrived home exhausted and talked through what had happened as if doing so might guide us through the following day. Then we woke up and resumed the routine of the parking garage and the ICU check-in desk and the twenty-four-hour Au Bon Pain, only to discover that, beyond those things, there was no routine at all, nothing whatsoever to help us prepare or plan. It was like trying to dress every morning for the weather in a nation we had never heard of.

Living through the death of someone you love is such an intimate act that, inevitably, the memory of it inheres in odd, specific things: the voicemail you left for your cousin that he will never hear; the television show that was on in the background when the phone with its terrible foreknowledge began to ring; the darkened windowpane in the front door, turning red and then blue and then red again from the police lights revolving silently outside it. Yet for all this variability, a kind of sameness shapes the experience of death for many of us today, because so much of it takes place in hospitals. A hundred thousand plots unfold in just one setting; it is as if we had all wandered into the same upsetting dream. And while a hospital can be, in many ways, a good place to die, it is a strange and difficult place to begin to mourn. In my many previous visits, I had always tried to temper any negative feelings I had about hospitals, because I knew that wonderful things happened in them, too—that all around me, lives were being saved, pain ameliorated, hope restored, babies born. And I had witnessed some of this myself. My niece, three pounds at birth, terrifying in her miniature perfection: a month in the neonatal intensive care unit gave her back to us, squalling, healthy, unblemished, miraculous. My father's pulmonary artery, mended at forty-five, again at sixty, barely so much as a scar paid either time for the price of all those extra years. I would forgive hospitals almost anything for such gifts as these.

And yet it was awful, awful and dismal, to sit in one day after day while my father was dying. It was cold almost all of the time; I begged the nurses for extra blankets and piled them, thin and white, in threes and fours on top of my mother, who sat in a vinyl recliner at my father's side, reading or dozing and holding his hand. There was a bench seat opposite the doorway, a metal chair against the wall; I stretched out on the one or sat in the other or stood up and looked out the window. It would have been boring if it hadn't also been horrible; something extremely urgent was happening, yet there was nothing whatsoever to do. The hours were interminable but infinitely subdivided—by a machine that beeped, a phlebotomist drawing blood, someone stopping by to check the levels in the bags of fluid that hung above my father's head. From time to time, a nurse would come in and everyone but my mother would discreetly leave the room, even though the need to do so had long since passed, modesty and privacy the least of anyone's worries anymore.

At other times, one of us would leave the room for some reason of our own, to make a phone call or go for a walk or head down to the cafeteria. In the elevator, thin old men in gowns gingerly escorted their own oxygen stands and mothers stood like weary sentinels behind their children's wheelchairs and brisk, busy doctors went respectfully silent while the doors opened up at one floor after another, the directory of destinations—NEUROLOGY, NEPHROLOGY, ONCOLOGY, RADIOLOGY, PATHOLOGY, PAIN MANAGEMENT, PEDIATRIC INTENSIVE CARE—offering up a vision of hell as thoroughgoing and carefully striated as the one Dante gave us. Some days, there was a woman stationed in the main lobby playing the harp, a gesture I found too cloying to be beautiful, even though the fountain just outside, which rippled in a similar way and was there for a similar reason, soothed and mesmerized me. In the hallway behind her there was a bookstore with a window display full of teddy bears, and beyond that the cafeteria, where, once a day or so, I wandered in circles around the offerings, trying and failing to summon any desire at all to eat.

On and on it went like this, day after day. I was conscious of how lucky we were that the era of limited visiting hours and one-guest-at-a-time policies had passed, just as I am conscious, writing this now, of how lucky we were that the era of no guests at all was not yet upon us: that my father did not sicken and die during the coronavirus pandemic, when everyone's grief was compounded by isolation—by the loss, on top of everything else, of the chance to sit with your loved one and say, "I'm right here." It was a privilege and a comfort to be at my father's side throughout his final weeks; if he was going to be confined to that room for so long, we wanted to be with one another, and with him.

Still, unless you work there, a hospital is no kind of place to spend so much time. Like a storefront church, its physical presence is at odds with its existential responsibilities. In an ICU, you are as aware of the brevity of life and the great looming precipice of eternity as Wordsworth was at Tintern Abbey, yet at the same time you are basically stuck in an airport. There is the same combination of impatience and impotence; the same constant proximity to strangers; the same unavoidable dependence on professionals either kindly or officious; the same long walk to unappealing, overpriced commerce; the same creeping exhaustion that enters, like a quality of the air, almost the moment you walk through the door; the same sense of temporal dislocation, of existing in some stranded time zone distinct from all those in the outside world. In our case, because my father's condition was so mysterious, there was also the sense of being on a layover in a distant city when your flight has been canceled and no further information is forthcoming—except that, instead of waiting for a plane, we were waiting for devastation or deliverance.

Here is another way that hospitals, in my experience, too seldom live up to their existential obligations: in all the time my father was in the ICU—heart rhythm erratic, kidneys failing, blood pressure dropping, white blood cell count soaring, barely responsive, neither eating nor drinking—the doctors assigned to his care suggested everything under the sun (a different combination of drugs, more dialysis, a spinal tap, a blood test to rule out a rare disease, an MRI of his heart and lungs) except that he was dying and that we could choose to let him do so in peace. Even when my mother and sister began asking point-blank about the odds of survival, and the odds in that case that he would emerge afterward with a life worth living, they refused to answer, or to say anything more than that it was a complex case and up to the family to make a decision—as if, despite having none of their medical knowledge, we were somehow better off arriving at one on our own than with their assistance.

I wish it had been otherwise; I wish that all doctors spoke honestly about death when it is imminent. But I can't wholly blame those who fail to do so, because, on my own, I would have served my father and my family just as poorly. I am badly built for the kind of wisdom required in extremis: I love life too much, am too willing to gamble on terrible odds, too inclined to hope against hope for more hope. But I knew my sister was right on the day when she sat down beside me and told me, very gently, that even if by drastic intervention my father could be brought back from his precarious place out there on the edge of the end, we would be getting, in all the ways that mattered to us, less of him, not more. And I wept with gratitude when, finally, two doctors who were not on my father's medical team but were simply his friends came by to see him and told us, when we asked, that if it were up to them, as people who also loved him very much, they would let him go.

And so, one afternoon, instead of continuing to try to stave off death, we unbarred the door and began to wait. It was a relief to watch a nurse bandage up the dialysis port in my father's arm, remove the many sticky-backed sensors with their tangle of wires from his skin, and detach him

from all his machines. She was infinitely gentle, with him
and with us, the last of a thousand kindnesses from the
nursing staff—all those blankets, all those compassionate
words, all those questions answered and doctors summoned
and extra chairs procured—before they transferred him to
hospice care. When she was done, the rest of us gathered up
our belongings and went down the hallway and up the elevator and settled, alongside my father, into his new and final
room.

It was smaller and simpler than the one in the ICU, and
much quieter. A few times a day, a nurse slipped in to check
on him, but otherwise, we were alone with our thoughts and
each other and, for one final spell, with my father. To my
surprise, I found it comforting to be with him during this
time, to sit by his side and hold his hand and watch his chest
rise and fall with a familiar little riffle of snore. It was not,
as they say, unbearably sad; on the contrary, it was bearably
sad—a tranquil, contemplative, lapping kind of sorrow. I
thought, as it turns out mistakenly, that what I was doing
during those days was making my peace with his death. But
I have learned since then that even one's unresponsive and
dying father is, in some extremely salient way, still alive.

And then, very early one morning, he was not. I remember the way my mind absented itself immediately, so that
the few cool syllables to which I had access seemed almost
to have formed outside of me: *so this is it*. I remember feeling simultaneously heavy and empty, like a steel safe with
nothing inside. I remember seeing my little niece place a letter she had written to her grandpa on his chest, where, for
all the long moments that I looked at it, it failed to move.
But what I remember most from those first hours after my
father died is watching my mother cradle the top of his bald

head in her hand. A wife holding her dead husband, without trepidation, without denial, without any possibility of being cared for in return, just for the chance to be tender toward him one last time: it was the purest act of love I'd ever seen. She looked bereft, beautiful, unimaginably calm. He did not yet look dead. He looked like my father. I could not stop picturing the way he used to push his glasses up onto his forehead to read. It struck me, right before everything else struck me much harder, that I should set them by his bed in case he needed them.

So BEGAN MY long sojourn in the Valley of Lost Things. Three weeks after my father died, I lost another family member, this one to cancer. Three weeks after that, in the tenth inning of the seventh game, my hometown baseball team lost the World Series—an outcome that wouldn't have particularly affected me if my father hadn't been such a passionate fan. One week later, Hillary Clinton, together with a little over half this nation's voters, lost the presidential election.

Like a dysfunctional form of love, which to some extent it is, grief has no boundaries; seldom during that difficult fall could I distinguish my distress over these other losses from my sadness about my father. I had maintained my composure during his memorial service, even while delivering the eulogy. But when the son of the deceased stood up to speak at the second funeral, I wept. Afterward, I couldn't shake the sense that another shoe was about to drop—that I would learn at any moment that someone else close to me had died. The morning after the election, I cried again, missing my refugee father, missing the future I had thought would unfold. In its place, other kinds of losses suddenly seemed imminent as well: of civil rights, personal safety, financial security, the foundational American values of respect for dissent and difference, the institutions and protections of democracy.

For weeks, I slogged on like this, through waves of both actual and imagined grief. I couldn't stop picturing catastrophes, both political and personal. I felt a rising fear whenever my mother didn't answer her phone, hated to see my sister board an airplane, could barely let my partner get in a car. "So many things seem filled with the intent / to be lost," Elizabeth Bishop wrote, and as much or more than my specific unhappiness, it was just that—the sheer quantity and inevitability of further suffering—that undid me.

Yet for all that I wanted to keep those I loved close, even their presence occasioned a certain amount of pain. One consequence of losing a parent—obvious enough, although it hadn't occurred to me beforehand—is that it reconfigures the rest of your family. All my life, it had been the four of us; to the extent that had ever changed, it had only been joyfully, in the direction of more. But part of mourning my father involved acclimating to a new family geometry, a triangle instead of a square. As a unit, we were smaller, differently balanced, and, at first, unavoidably sadder.

A large part of that sadness was the terrible severing of my father from my mother. I had spent a decade worrying about him, but almost immediately after he died, as if by some law of conservation of anxiety, my fears redirected themselves toward my mother. These were not, for the most part, about her physical health, which was considerably better than his had been. Instead, what worried me was the gaping emptiness in her life after a half century of my father's steadfast presence. "I can't imagine her without him," people routinely say of those who have lost a spouse, but my problem was that I imagined it constantly. As often as not, in those early days, my own grief took the form of being undone by the thought of my mother going about her days alone.

Eventually, I realized that I had underestimated my mother, as adult children so often do. She really did miss my father as much as I feared, but I soon found that she grieved as she had always done everything: patiently and tenderly, with a remarkable ability to accept the worst days as inevitable and a remarkable will to live as well as possible on all the rest. Her grace and fortitude awed me, not least because I kept demonstrating the opposite qualities, literally: in the aftermath of my father's death, I grew uncharacteristically clumsy and prone to ailment and injury. I ran a low-grade fever for the better part of three weeks, suffered a pinched nerve, pulled a hamstring, fell twice for no reason, was plagued by unexplained tooth pain, and, worst of all, one terrible morning while making coffee, overturned an entire carafe of boiling water onto my forearm. A psychologist would say that some part of me was unconsciously trying to make manifest my emotional pain, and I'm sure that's true. Yet at the time, all these mishaps and maladies felt less like an ongoing psychosomatic calamity than like a pervasive loss of balance, as if I were no longer on familiar terms with the basic physical operations of my body and the world.

Whatever caused them, the cumulative effect of these various debilities was to make me feel tremendously old. Or maybe that's backward—maybe I incurred all those debilities because I already felt old. Grief of any kind will age you, partly from exhaustion but chiefly from the confrontation with mortality: to feel old (as distinct from actually being old, which can be a perfectly contented state) is to feel that both your days and your remaining quantity of joy are diminishing. But grief over a parent will also age you because it pitches you forward an entire life stage. Losing my father felt like advancing one notch in the march of generations—like taking, all at once, one very large step toward oblivion. I seemed overnight to have become middle-aged, which was strange, because my sadness also sometimes made me feel very young, still needing my father and not yet fit to be left without him. In a peculiar, circular way, I felt old because I felt like a child, at a time when I also felt that I had been a child so very long ago.

Disoriented, anxious, injured, ill: given all this, it is hardly surprising that, for some time after my father died, I was also spectacularly useless. I had lost, along with everything else, all motivation; day after day, I did as close as humanly possible to nothing. In part, that was because action felt like acceleration, and I dreaded getting further from the time when my father was still alive. But it was also because, after all the obvious tasks of mourning were completed— the service over, the clothing donated, the thank-you cards written—I had no idea what else to do. Although I had spent almost a decade worrying about losing my father, I had never once thought about what would come next. Like a heart, my imagination had always stopped at the moment of death.

Now, obliged to carry onward through time, I realized that I didn't know how. I found some consolation in poetry, but otherwise, for the first time in my life, I did not care to read. Nor could I bring myself to write. In theory, I had a full-time magazine job, but I worked from home, on a schedule of my own choosing. That was a luxury I had previously cherished, but in the early days of mourning, it left me unmoored; even after the tactful post-death pause had passed and obligations and deadlines began crowding in on me, I found myself too drained and preoccupied to focus. Day after day, I turned my laptop on and stared at it for a while and turned it off again, feeling a profound kinship with its empty screen. I knew that for emotional as well as professional and financial reasons, I needed to start writing again; I knew that I needed to go to sleep at a decent hour and wake up at one, too; I knew that I needed to eat right and reach out to friends and call up a therapist I hadn't spoken to in years. I knew everything I should be doing, yet knew of nothing at all that I wanted to do.

It was my father, predictably, who gave me the word for the one thing I *was* doing. In his lifetime, he had possessed an astonishing vocabulary, one so nuanced and capacious that even when it failed him, it succeeded. Once, after I somehow came across the word "circumjoviating" and had to look it up—it means "orbiting around Jupiter"—I challenged him to define it. He thought for perhaps five seconds, then guessed, logically and sublimely: "avoiding God." I have used it that way ever since then—for what other word so concisely describes the experience of ducking one's deity or conscience or responsibilities? Like so much of what I got from my father, it is a gift of ethics inside a gift of language. And so it came back to me after he died, when I sat there impassively and watched it start to define me: avoiding work, avoiding books, avoiding time, avoiding joy, avoiding reality.

I did not exactly feel lost, as my father was unto me. I felt *at a loss*—a strange turn of phrase, as if loss were a place in the physical world, a kind of reverse oasis or Bermuda Triangle where the spirit fails and the compass needle spins. I stretched out for as long as I could the small acts that felt manageable and right (calling my mother and sister, curling up with my partner, playing with the cats), but these alone could not fill up the days. Every night I went to bed exhausted and slept for an absurd number of hours, slept in a way I had only done before when seriously ill. Every morning I woke up in the grip of two opposite fears: that my time on earth was streaming away behind me with unbearable swiftness; that another day loomed up in front of me with leaden interminability. Not since the age of eight, when I was still learning to master boredom, had life struck me so much as simply a problem of what to do.

IT WAS DURING this time of torpor and drift that I began to go out looking for my father. Because I find peace and clarity in nature, I did this searching outside, sometimes while walking, sometimes while out on a run. (Running was the one thing I kept doing during those long doldrums after my father died. I knew enough about its role in my life—as body maintainer, mind clearer, mood regulator—that I didn't dare stop.) Like so much else during those difficult early days of grief, these expeditions had a hazy, half-formed quality. They came about without any planning or perceptible decision, as if I knew that they wouldn't bear the weight of serious thought—which they would not, because nothing in my understanding of death suggested that they would succeed. I don't believe that the essence of each of us endures unchanged after we die, or that the dead can commune with the living. But grief makes reckless cosmologists of us all, and I thought it possible, in an impossible kind of way, that if I went out looking, I might find myself, however briefly or inexplicably, in my father's company again.

I have subsequently learned that this searching behavior, as it is called, is common among the bereaved. It is so common, in fact, that the psychologist John Bowlby, a contemporary of Elisabeth Kübler-Ross's, regarded the second stage of grief, after shock and numbness, as "yearning and searching." And yet, before my father died, I myself had never engaged in it—perhaps because, until then, my dead had always saved me the trouble by coming to look for me. When I was fourteen, my maternal great-grandmother died in her sleep at the age of ninety-three. For as long as I had known her, she had been the very soul of gentleness, but some months later, when I was slouched on our living room couch reading a book, I heard her voice just behind me, telling me sharply to sit up straight and cross my legs, please. Twenty-three years later, her daughter, my grandmother, died at ninety-five. She had definitely not been the soul of gentleness, but she was an excellent grandparent, fierce and smart and interesting, and so it was characteristic, if also extremely startling, when I stood up one night to go to bed, having decided to give up on some piece of writing that was going badly, and heard her say behind me, "That's a terrible idea."

My most memorable experiences of this kind, however, began the year I turned sixteen, following the shocking loss of one of my closest friends. One evening after school we talked on the phone for a while, as we often did; hours later, she was murdered. It was sudden and shattering and I was

still very young, and the combination made her death exceptionally difficult to absorb. For years afterward, I had dreams
that she had faked it, or that we had both been subjected to
an elaborate hoax. I suspect it was for this same reason—the
near impossibility of believing that she was gone—that, for
quite a while, I felt her presence with some regularity. The
first time, I was walking home from school when I heard
her say my name, sounding simultaneously exasperated and
encouraging, as if in cheerful rebuke to my grief. Far more
strangely, I was twice jolted into the conviction that I had
encountered her again in an altered but unmistakable form:
first as a caterpillar and then, much later and even more improbably, as a plastic bag—or, rather, as the breeze inside it
that sent it tumbling past me on a dusty back road late one
summer afternoon. I hadn't been thinking of my friend at
all that day; ten years had passed since she had died. Yet the
moment I saw the bag, I laughed out loud. For no apparent
reason—surely nothing could be further from our customary notions of visitation and rebirth—it filled me with instant, overwhelming recognition.

Only years later did I learn that experiences like these are
also common among the grieving. "I never thought Michiko
would come back / after she died," the poet Jack Gilbert
wrote of his wife in "Alone." "It is strange that she has returned / as somebody's dalmatian." When they involve seeing, hearing, or sensing the dead, such encounters are called
bereavement hallucinations, and somewhat more than half
of people report having experienced them. (That percentage
is even higher among the widowed, and it rises in tandem
with the length of the marriage.) No one knows what causes
them, but, as the neurologist Oliver Sacks once observed,
they have something in common with the hallucinations ex-

perienced by people in solitary confinement, people who have recently gone blind, and people who are exposed exclusively to monotonous landscapes, as on ocean crossings or long polar voyages. In all these cases, and perhaps in bereavement as well, the abrupt withdrawal of familiar sensory input leads the mind to fill in what has always been there before but is suddenly missing.

Plenty of people who have experienced bereavement hallucinations don't believe in any kind of afterlife, and I am one of them. Vivid as mine were, they neither comported with my understanding of death nor, strange as this may seem, changed it. If they brought me nearer to any kind of faith, it was only to one I have always had, in the infinite mysteries of the human mind. In every case, they were welcome and startling and also somehow slightly comic, yet they felt far more earthly than holy. I never sensed that I was in the presence of anything either angelic or ghostly, or that the curtain had somehow thinned between this world and another. But I also didn't experience these interactions as happening inside my own head. The voices, in particular—of my grandmother chiding me or my friend saying my name—had a kind of exteriority entirely unlike thoughts or memories or even dreams. To the extent that I could categorize them at all, they seemed to belong less to the uncanny than to its opposite: to the deeply familiar, as if they were a form I hadn't known that love could take until I experienced grief.

It was this comforting rush of familiarity that I was seeking when I went out looking for my father: since he hadn't come to me in the weeks after his death, I thought perhaps that I could go to him. The first time I tried—it was late one October afternoon, gray and cheerless, with the first intimation of winter in the air—I turned around after five minutes. I have seldom attempted anything that felt so futile. It brought back a memory from when I was nine or ten years old and had set about experimenting with telekinesis. I succeeded that October day at summoning my father about as well as I had succeeded back then in sliding a pencil off my desk from across the room—which is to say that not only didn't it work, I couldn't imagine any mechanism, mental state, physical act, expression of commitment, or admission of need that could possibly make it work, or even count as practice. And yet, in both cases, I kept trying.

It didn't work the next time, either; it has never worked. I don't know why I haven't felt my father's presence since his death, as I have with other people I've loved and mourned. I do know, though, that I have no business feeling surprised and denied when the universe behaves in accordance with my own understanding of it. I have always regarded this to be one of the inviolable terms of our existence: the people we love cease to exist upon death, as definitively as water flows out of a glass when you overturn it.

I know that not everyone shares this conviction. Some people feel watched over by their late loved ones in this lifetime, and some are confident that they will encounter them again in the next one. But I also know that this sense of absolute loss is not just the burden of agnostics and atheists. After his wife, Joy Davidman, died of breast cancer, C. S. Lewis, that most devout and knowledgeable of Christians, wrote a slim and devastating little book called *A Grief Observed*. He published it under a pseudonym, knowing that it might trouble his more pious admirers—not because it was blasphemous or because he had ceased to believe in God but because the explication of faith it contained was almost entirely lacking in the usual comforts. "Talk to me about the truth of religion and I'll listen gladly," he wrote. "Talk to me about the duty of religion and I'll listen submissively. But don't come talking to me about the consolations of religion or I shall suspect that you don't understand." The self unaltered by death, the past restored, a glorious reunion on some shining farther shore: that's "all out of bad hymns and lithographs," Lewis continued. "There's not a word of it in the Bible." Nothing in Scripture promised him that he would be reunited with his wife after his own death, and he felt sure that he would not be, because he felt sure that the woman he longed for no longer existed. "I look up at the night sky," he wrote: "Is anything more certain than that in all those vast times and spaces, if I were allowed to search them, I should nowhere find her face, her voice, her touch?" Between his late wife and himself, he felt only "the locked door, the iron curtain, the vacuum, absolute zero."

Thus have I felt about my father since he died. Never in all the time I spent searching did I find the slightest trace of him. In the years since then, I have tried in quiet moments to summon some suggestion of his presence but have felt no stirring whatsoever, no sign at all beyond my own mind and memories. Being his daughter now is like holding one of those homemade tin-can telephones with no tin can on the other end of the string. His absence is total; where there was him, there is nothing.

TRADITIONALLY, MOURNING IS a public and a structured process. We attend viewings and funerals and memorial services, cover our mirrors, sit shiva for a week, recite the kaddish for at least a month, wear black for a year and a day. Grief, by contrast, is a private experience, unconstrained by ritual or time. Popular wisdom will tell you that it comes in stages—denial, anger, bargaining, depression, acceptance— and that may be true. But the Paleozoic era also came in stages—Cambrian, Ordovician, Silurian, Devonian, Carboniferous, Permian—and it lasted two hundred and ninety million years.

Like anything that goes on for too long, grief is (I don't know why people don't talk about this aspect of it more often) unbelievably boring. I don't mean in its earliest days, when the sorrow is too acute and the overall rearrangement of life too recent to allow for anything like tedium. Eventually, though, as you grow accustomed to its constant companionship, the monotony sets in. I can't recall exactly how long after my father's death this happened for me, because mourning also played havoc with my sense of time, but I think several months must have passed when the grief that had sloshed around turbulently inside me ebbed into a stagnant pool. It made life seem extremely dull and it made me seem extremely dull and, above all, it became, itself, unbelievably wearying. I remember declaring out loud one day how sick I was of it—of the blanched, lethargic, dismal endlessness of grieving. It seemed an affront to my father, who was among the least boring people ever to live, as well as a waste of time, which, as his death had just reminded me in the strongest possible terms, is a precious and finite gift. But I could no more will away the dreariness than I could will back him.

To make matters worse, this boredom offered no protection from the capriciousness of grief. We think of "boring" as synonymous with "predictable," but I found the process of grieving to be simultaneously volatile and tedious. In this, it resembled the experience of being in the hospital while my father was dying; the emotions were enormous and erratic, the days cramped and repetitive. Like stress, depression, and physical pain, grief wears us down by the mere fact of always being there. Each day you wake up and the mortgage is unpaid, each day you wake up and your back hurts, each day you wake up and your father is dead. But every climate has its weather, and on top of this bleakness, my grief felt chaotic—affected so constantly and subtly by so many different factors that its behavior at any given moment could shock me.

Some days, for instance, I would find myself feeling genuinely, deeply, gloriously fine. I recall in particular returning from one bright, cold winter run full of the exuberant conviction that I was okay, everything was okay, I was grateful for my father's life and at peace with his death and aware that he had given me everything I could possibly need to go on without him—all of which was completely true but, as a mid-grief mood, unsustainable. Other days, I felt like a ghostly simulacrum of fine: calm, blank, functional, feelingless. Still other days, I was filled with a strange, undirected anxiety, as if part of my mind had forgotten that my father had died and was casting around with increasing dread trying to figure out what was wrong. I felt like I was waiting for the thing that had already happened, and it made me jumpy and distracted. ("No one ever told me that grief felt so like fear," C. S. Lewis wrote. "The same fluttering in the stomach, the same restlessness, the yawning.")

Another thing I felt, albeit thinly, was anger. It is common enough for the bereft to experience fits of rage—at oneself, at God, at the injustice of the world, at the dead for dying, at a total stranger for having the nerve to still have a living spouse or child, at the sudden unbearable indignity and release of whacking your head on an open cabinet door. I had felt this kind of irrational, surging fury in the past while grieving, but after my father died, I found myself subject only to its lackluster cousin: irritability. Like sleep deprivation, grief makes it hard to maintain equilibrium, and regrettably often after my father died, I felt myself becoming testy and difficult. Minor things that would not normally have bothered me occasioned a hot spike of infuriation: the grocery store clerk needing to summon a manager to complete a transaction when I was in a hurry, my mother forgetting to turn down the television in the background when she and I were on the phone. Even in the midst of those moments, I knew that the ostensible object of my aggravation was not the issue. I was just frustrated with the new terms of my life—with the fact that my father was gone, and with the necessity of grieving him. "It's so annoying that my father died," I announced one day, which was completely true, although I had meant to say, "It's so annoying that my phone died."

Of all the ways that grief affected me, I liked this one the least. It paid poor tribute to the loss that caused it, and it left me in a strange, self-devouring mood, minor but with a vicious existential edge. Among the many emotional reactions I had to my father's death, it felt furthest from the root state of sorrow—although, in my experience, sorrow often feels surprisingly distant when we grieve. Before I had ever experienced it, I'd assumed that grief was a form of sadness, basically synonymous with it but more extreme. And maybe, in some subterranean way, that's true; maybe all the other things I felt along the way—anxiety and exhaustion and irritability and lassitude—were just secondary phenomena, produced by and more accessible than the sorrow they obscured. In the end, though, it makes no difference, because, by common consensus, it is all these other things that the bereft most often feel. Ever since Kübler-Ross proposed her taxonomy of grief (originally to describe the experience of facing one's own death but now widely used for those in mourning), people have been debating the validity and universality of her five stages and proposing additional ones: shock, pain, guilt, reflection, reconstruction, hope. Yet neither the old model nor any of the new ones include sadness as a defining feature of grief.

That surprising omission accurately reflects my own experience. Obviously I often was and sometimes still am deeply sad about my father's death. I can remember whole days when sorrow pooled around me, so palpable and unadulterated that the only answer to questions about how I was doing or what was going on was "I'm just sad." And I can remember other days when a more dire form of that feeling would overtake me—the thing I thought grief would always be like, a tidal wave roaring up to swamp me with the undiminished measure of my loss. But neither one, the pool or the wave, were regular components of my grief.

Instead, I found sadness to be, in every sense, a vulnerable thing, a small neutral nation on a bellicose continent whose borders were constantly overrun by more aggressive emotions. I also found it to be strangely furtive, strangely insubordinate; it went into hiding easily and could not be roused against its will. I could think about my father, I could miss my father, I could love my father, but I could not make myself sad about him when and where I chose, any more than I could tickle myself or compel myself to fall in love. It rose

up in me of its own accord, for reasons I could only sometimes deduce even after the fact, or it was provoked by one
or another cause entirely external to me. These were seldom
the predictable triggers of holidays or my parents' anniversary or the necessity of attending a funeral, all of which I
could brace myself to experience. By contrast, the things
that undid me were almost always unexpected and generally
oblique—as on the day a little over a year after my father
died when, in an instant, the words on my laptop blurred
over in front of me and a bite of bagel turned to chalk in my
mouth because, sitting in a café in Manhattan, I overheard
a man say to his lunch companion, "I wish my daughter
would call me more often."

I sometimes yearned for more moments like that, moments when my sorrow ran through me like a river at night,
dark and clear, untainted by any more insidious emotion.
Yet such things aren't responsive to our wishes. If we could
summon sorrow, we could banish it, but the whole lesson
grief teaches us is that we are not the ones in control. Books
and manuals and websites about bereavement are full of advice about how to "move through grief," and it is true that
there are better and worse ways to cope with the death of
someone you love. I tried hard to steer to the side of
better—to not mourn alone, not remain too much indoors,
not numb or deny the pain, not neglect too often or for too
long my family and friends and body and work and the
events and needs of the rest of the world. I am sure it all
helped, if only by keeping things from getting worse. But
even in the midst of those acts of self-care, it never felt to me
like I was moving through grief, with all the striding agency
that phrase implies. It felt like grief was moving through
me—like it was a force outside my influence, entirely wild,

no more swayed by my will than a mountain lion or a storm. Like all truly wild things, it was overwhelming and sometimes frightening up close but strangely compelling from a little distance, stark and awesome in the old sense of the word; and when it went away again, especially as the amount of time between its unpredictable appearances lengthened, I sometimes longed, perversely, for its return.

Most people, I think, are at least a little afraid of ceasing to grieve. I know that I was. However terrible our sorrow may be, we understand that it is made in the image of love, that it shares the characteristics of the person we mourn. Maybe there was a day in your life when you were brought to your knees by a faded blue ball cap or a tote bag full of knitting supplies or the sound of a Brahms piano concerto. For my part, I have been moved to tears by a pile of my father's button-down shirts, amassed in my parents' bedroom awaiting donation; by a polished wooden wall clock, identical to one he had in his law office when I was young, that shocked me with how much of my childhood it suddenly summoned; by a battered edition of *Middlemarch,* creased down the middle where its spine had been broken (my father bent his paperbacks in half to read them as reflexively and contentedly as New Yorkers fold a piece of pizza before eating it); and by a pale green packet of Wrigley's chewing gum, half its little paper sleeves emptied of their silver foil. But here is the curious part: all of these things, which grief wielded like weapons, are actually quite wonderful to me— strange, specific, welcome returnees from their long exile in the land of the past. Part of what makes grief so seductive, then, is that it seems to offer us what life no longer can: an ongoing, emotionally potent connection to the dead. And so it is easy to feel that once that bleak gift is gone, the person we love will somehow be more gone, too.

Thus our strange relationship with the pain of grief. In the early days, we wish only for it to end; later on, we fear that it will. And when it finally does begin to ease, it also does not, because, at first, feeling better can feel like loss, too. "The trees are coming into leaf," the poet Philip Larkin once wrote,

> Like something almost being said;
> The recent buds relax and spread,
> Their greenness is a kind of grief.

This type of circular mourning, the grieving of grief itself, is perfectly normal and possibly inevitable yet also misguided and useless. There is no honor in feeling awful and no betrayal in feeling better, and no matter how dark and salted and bitter cold your grief may be, it will never preserve anything about the person you mourn. Despite how it sometimes feels, it has never kept anyone alive, not even in memory. If anything, it keeps them dead: eventually, if you cannot stop mourning, the person you love will come to be made only of grief.

THE LOSS OF someone you love is too immense an experience to take in all at once. Only belatedly does it begin to reveal itself in its fullness, after the terrible king tide of grief has receded, leaving all kinds of strange things behind. I would not have predicted, for instance, that of everything about those final weeks in the hospital, what would stay with me most is my father's silence. Although it baffled and upset me at the time, it did not command as large a share of my emotional attention as it does now. There was so much else going on, so many critical systems of his body in crisis, so many hours spent talking through seemingly pressing issues that, in the end, would never matter—would he be on dialysis for the rest of his life? did we need to look into long-term care?—that his mysterious inability to speak did not seem like the most urgent of his problems. No one, after all, has ever died of silence.

And yet if anyone ever could die that way, it might well have been my effusive, communicative, multilingual father. His silence was so unlike him, so contrary to the whole spirit of his existence, that in retrospect I feel I should have known what it portended. Instead, I did everything I could to counterbalance it. Together with the rest of my family, I sat by my father's bed and talked to him, recited him poetry, called up music on my laptop and filled his hospital room with Tchaikovsky and Chopin and Beethoven's "Ode to Joy." All the things he loved, all the remarkable things people have forged out of ideas and emotion and sound: I hoped then, and still hope now, that he could hear them and know them for what they were. Failing that, I hope he could hear them and find them wonderful all over again, wonderful the way they were the first time he encountered them. Failing that, I hope he was at peace.

My father's familiar brown eyes, following me mutely around a hospital room: this is always what I think of now when I think of the time he was dying. I wonder often what was going on behind them. It is impossible to say whether his silence reflected a deeper breakdown, the slow coming

apart of thought itself, or if it was simply the result of a
breach in his relationship with the world—some barrier de-
scending or some longstanding connection being severed.
Was the silence inner as well as outer? Or was it, for him,
like looking through a window in a lighted room at night,
the interior illuminated, everything outside shadowy and
difficult to see? I don't know, and I don't know why I am so
troubled by not knowing. In the end, we leave the world and
we leave ourselves, and I suppose it doesn't really matter in
which order. I could not even tell you which of the two I
think is lonelier.

In Roman mythology, one of the goddesses of death was
named Tacita: the silent one. Ovid reports that, to propiti-
ate her on the Day of the Dead, the devout sacrificed to her
a fish with its mouth sewn shut. It was an apt offering, to an
apt deity. Death sews every mouth shut; everything about it
defies language. The dead themselves can't speak, and the
living can't speak firsthand about dying, and even finding
appropriate words for mourning can be extremely difficult.
You learn something about grief from grieving, but it is a
lonely, threadbare knowledge, hard to describe, bespoke in
almost every detail. I was vexed to discover, after my father
died, how useless I was when called upon to console someone else in the face of death, how almost impossible it was
to say anything at all that, in accuracy or helpfulness, could
best the average platitude. Even when I was talking with my
sister, whose sorrow pains me more than my own and who
is the only other person on the planet to grieve my father *as*
a father—even then, I don't think I ever once said anything
remotely comforting or useful. What comes to mind now is
being on the phone with her one afternoon some months
after his death and, into the silence following a sad acknowl-

edgment of how much we both missed him, saying only "Ugh."

It was a representative syllable. *Ugh, ach, argh, oy:* those inarticulate, literally meaningless little interjections are the equivalent, on a less dire day, of moaning and keening. Even when grief doesn't level us, it mocks our ability to put the world into words. The stark fact at the heart of it—gone, gone, gone, gone—is at once too obvious to merit saying and too terrible to say as often and indiscriminately as we feel it. Tearing our hair, gnashing our teeth, rending our clothes: the impulse may be there, but the action is generally inhibited by the helpful but comically mismatched dictates of polite society. You go to work, you go to the baby shower, you say that you are hanging in there, thanks for asking. And all the while you are suppressing the news that someone you love has undergone that everyday, unimaginable passage out of this world.

I suppose that is the other reason why my father's silence has stayed with me: because it *is* still with me. It was a foretaste of the permanent one to come, a loss so total that for a while I did not understand its real scope. And then one night, during that early stretch of grief when I could find solace only in poetry, my partner sat me down and read me "Crossing Brooklyn Ferry." In it, Walt Whitman leans against the railing of a ship, just north of where my father first looked out on New York Harbor, and exalts in all that he sees. So expansive is Whitman's vision that it includes not just the piers and sails and reeling gulls but everyone else who makes the crossing, too: all those who stood at the railing watching before his birth, all those presently watching around him, and all those who will be there watching after his death—which, in the poem, he doesn't so much foresee as, through a wild, craning omniscience, look back on. "Just as you feel when you look on the river and sky, so I felt," he admonishes, kindly.

And just like that, mid-poem, mid-grief, my understanding of loss revealed itself as terribly narrow. What I had been missing about my father—talking with him, laughing with him, sharing my thoughts and feelings in order to hear his own in response—was life as it looked filtered through him, held up and considered against his inner lights. But the most important thing that had vanished when he died, I realized in that instant, is wholly unavailable to me: life as it looked *to* him, life as we all live it, from the inside out. All of my memories can't add up to a single moment of what it was like to be him, and all of my loss pales beside his own. Like Whitman's, my father's love of life had been exuberant, exhaustive; he must have hated, truly hated, to leave it behind—not just the people he adored, but all of it, sea to shining sea.

It is breathtaking, the extinguishing of a consciousness. Viewed from any distance at all, it is, I know, the most common of all losses, repeated every hour of every day since the dawn of history. But viewed up close, it is shocking, a whole universe flashing out of existence. I lost my father; my father lost everything. That is the absolute loss that his silence in the hospital foretold: the end of the mind, the end of the self, the end of being a part of all of this—the harbor, the city, the poetry, the world. "He became his admirers," a different poet, W. H. Auden, wrote of Yeats when the latter died. Now we who loved my father are all that is left of him.

———

THERE IS A chair in my sister's living room that my father used to claim as his own every November when our family descended on her house for Thanksgiving. He would settle into it shortly after arriving and occupy it more or less continuously until the time came to leave, give or take meals and the occasional stroll down the hall to his granddaughter's room for bedtime stories and animated discussions about current affairs in the land of dolls and stuffed animals. This was toward the end of his life—in earlier years, my parents had hosted the holiday themselves—when, between poor balance, a bad back, and time served, my father had been permanently discharged from kitchen duties. "I have become," he once declared, after the act of standing up from the chair to help out had triggered a chorus of voices ordering him to sit back down, "an adornment."

Neither in the pejorative nor in the complimentary sense was my father ever what you would call ornamental. Still, he did improve every room he ever entered. At Thanksgiving, he would sit there all day in his chair, not exactly holding court and not exactly holding forth yet nonetheless seeming like our own private philosopher-king. When the rest of us were lounging around in the living room with him, he would play with great gusto his many overlapping roles: father, grandfather, scholar, wiseacre, fielder of questions, benevolent inquisitor, master of ceremonies. When we were busy cooking or working or out for a walk, he would push his glasses up onto his forehead and return to whichever book he was reading—"*Hebrew for Ancient People*," he once joked when I asked him, an effortless double entendre.

"Where there was him, there is nothing," I wrote of my father earlier, and that is true, with the caveat that "nothing" is not a neutral blankness. In the lane behind my house, there is a tree where I once saw an owl; now, every time I pass it, I look up automatically. That is something like the nothingness left behind after death: the place in the tree where the owl is not. From the first Thanksgiving after my father died, I have never once looked at that chair without remembering my father in it. And it is not just the chair. My father is not in my life in the same way he used to be in my life: everywhere and unmistakably. I imagine this is true for almost everyone who has lost someone they love. To be bereft is to live with the constant presence of absence.

This sounds upsetting, and at first it is. From almost the moment he died, I understood that my father, who never wanted anything more than for his daughters to be happy, would not want me to remember him in sorrow. And yet for a long time afterward, my world turned into, in both senses, a negative space: a map of where my father was not. That map did not just include all those places, like the chair, where he had always been. It also included all the places where he would never be. Not long after his death, I fell to talking with an older friend, who told me that his own father was still alive, at ninety-four. I can't remember what I said in response, and I don't know how I kept the conversation going, because all I could think was: *twenty more years.* I could have had my father in my life for another two decades—an unfathomably long extension, a literal generation of more time with him.

This kind of temporal reckoning is a common part of grieving. No matter when your loved ones die, there will always be a litany of things they did not live long enough to do: attend your graduation, dance at your wedding, see the house you bought, see the life you built, read the book you wrote, meet your children. Even if those future occurrences are wonderful in themselves, the thought of them after a death can be distressing. Grief confuses us by spinning us around to face backward, because memories are all we have left, but of course it isn't the past we mourn when someone dies; it's the future. That's what I realized while talking with my friend—that everything that happened in my life from that point on would be something else my father would not see.

It takes a long time to be done grieving, and even longer to know it. The periodicity of grief is too unreliable and the overall condition too chameleon to track with any certainty. Are you still mourning or just in a lousy mood? Have you crossed that faint boundary that marks the end of bereavement and the beginning of sorrow, an emotion you may feel on and off for the rest of your days? It is very difficult to say, especially because even when the worst has passed, or seems to have passed, there is nothing to prevent its return. Grief has an appalling recidivism rate, and it is common to find yourself back in it long past the point when you thought you were truly, thoroughly done. Still, for almost everyone, it really does fade away eventually. At some point, always retroactively, you look around your life and realize that it is gone.

The same is not true, however, for all the absences left behind by the death of someone you love. These just start to feel different, filled up as they finally are with something other than grief. I still notice, almost daily, all the places where my father is missing. I come upon them in photographs and in books that I'm reading, in the sound of my own sentences and the shape of my thoughts, in my mother and my sister, in my own face in the mirror, in the familiar sight of his wallet—safe now, as it never was with him—in my top dresser drawer. Some of these absences make me grateful, for who my father was and for the excuse to pause and spend a moment thinking of him. Some still have a melancholy, twilight feel. Some, like that chair, are a kind of commonplace memorial, a candle I don't have to light because it is always bright with him. Collectively, all of them serve to make the world a little less incomplete than it would otherwise be. They are still here, unlike him, and I assume they always will be, as enduring as the love that made them. This is the fundamental paradox of loss: it never disappears.

II.

Found

Here is a true story, very dear to my heart, about an eleven-year-old boy named Billy who was almost hit by a falling star. It happened one Sunday evening, in the summertime. After church, he sat down to lunch with his parents, and after that, he walked across a pasture and a cornfield to the Johnson farm. Roger Johnson was Billy's age, and for the two of them, summer Sundays were themselves a kind of field—broad and open, no adults watching over them, no school day looming up in front of them, no boundary to the day but the natural one of darkness. They played marbles; they climbed trees; they held corncob battles, using as ammunition the ones that always littered the ground. When those battles escalated, they scavenged in sheds and scrap piles, nailed a board between two saplings, stretched a bicycle tube across it, and declared the contraption a rocket launcher. Only when the birds grew raucous and the sky began to empty of light did Billy say his goodbyes and head home to do the milking.

The world is enormous in childhood. Even a modest suburban backyard contains its secret dangers and kingdoms; in the place Billy grew up, where a hundred acres regularly separated one neighbor from another, a walk home could span epochs and civilizations. The only thing larger than the land was the sky, obliged as it was to fill up all the space that the ground, which stretched almost perfectly flat from horizon to horizon, did not. Some days, he and Roger, sent to take the cows across the road, would lie down in the pasture with them and watch the clouds change overhead: a solitary dragon unfurling its tail, a lion leaning back on its haunches, a dark gray expanse like the ocean in bad weather, moving fast but furrowed as neatly as new plowing. Some nights, after his chores were done, Billy would sit alone behind the barn and watch the stars come out, one by one at first, and then in groups, and then in vast crowds, ten million strangers amassing with their torches in some other field incomprehensibly far away.

On this night, though, the sky was just starting to darken at its distant edge and the first stars were barely visible when Billy, who was still making his way home, turned around. In later years, he could never say exactly what made him do so—maybe just a whim, the impulse to walk backward for a while, as kids will do, or maybe a movement on the edge of his vision, or maybe a noise he didn't recognize. You can't hear a nearby meteorite while it is falling, any more than you can hear an apple falling from a tree. You can, however, hear the earth reacting to its descent from on high. So intense is the electromagnetic energy generated by meteorites that when it is absorbed by other objects—trees, fence posts, eyeglasses, hair—they heat up and expand, producing all kinds of strange sounds. Witnesses to meteorite falls have described hearing whistling, crackling, rumbling, hissing, sizzling, and a boom like the report of a cannon. Because that intense energy can also produce changes in air pressure, some physicists and planetary scientists believe that even people who hear nothing can sometimes "sense" a meteorite falling.

Whatever made him do it, when Billy turned around, something was hurtling downward out of the sky. It was small and dark and heading straight for him; alarmed, he turned and ran. When he finally stopped and looked again, the something was gone. He retraced his steps and tried to find it, but the longer he looked, the less light there was to see by, until finally he gave up and walked the rest of the way home through the gathering darkness. The next day, though, he went out again and, although he didn't know what he was looking for until he spotted it—and then he knew it right away: starkly out of place in the ordinary soil, smooth and exceptionally heavy in his two hands, thrilling as the infinite universe out of which it had fallen—he found it.

What an astonishing thing it is to find something. Children, who excel at it—chiefly because the world is still so new to them that they can't help but notice it—understand this, and automatically delight in it. You may hear a joyful shout of "Mom, come look what I found!" even when the thing in question is a dead banana slug on the front step. And they are right to feel this way. Finding is usually rewarding and sometimes exhilarating: a reunion with something old or an encounter with something new, a happy meeting between ourselves and some previously missing or mysterious bit of the cosmos.

A list of such meetings could fill volumes far larger than this one, because finding, like losing, is an enormous category, bursting with seemingly unrelated contents, from gold doubloons to God. We can find things like pencils in couch cushions and things like new planets in distant solar systems and things that aren't things at all: inner peace, old elementary school classmates, the solution to a problem. We can find things that were never missing, except from our own lives (as when we find a new job or a hole-in-the-wall barbecue joint), and we can find things so deeply hidden that almost no one else thought to look for them (as when we find glial cells or quarks).

Still, for all this variety, finding always takes one of two forms. The first is recovery: we can find something we previously lost. The second is discovery: we can find something we've never seen before. Recovery essentially reverses the impact of loss. It is a return to the status quo, a restoration of order to our world. Discovery, by contrast, *changes* our world. Instead of giving something back to us, it gives us something new.

Both of those outcomes sound wonderful, but neither kind of finding consistently makes good on that promise. Recovering a trouser sock that's been missing for fifteen wash cycles might bring some satisfaction—a kind of triumphant relief that is really just the end of irritation—but it doesn't leave anyone feeling fortunate or awestruck. Worse, sometimes we discover things that we wish we had not. A radiologist examining an X-ray detects the dark shadow of cancer; a son researching his genetic history learns that his father had children with another woman. But these are exceptions to a reasonably robust rule: for the most part, finding is as pleasing as losing is not.

Sometimes, in fact, it is more than pleasing; certain finds completely change our lives. Many factors made the death of my father difficult, but one thing above all others made it bearable: the year before he died, I fell in love. Most of what follows is an account of that experience. But just as every grief narrative is a reckoning with loss, every love story is a chronicle of finding, the private history of an extraordinary discovery. And so, much as my father's death made me wonder about the relationship between large losses and small ones, falling for someone made me think about what finding love has in common with the broader act of finding anything at all.

I have already mentioned one of the most important features of that broader act: finding something is almost always pleasurable. This is obvious enough when the thing we find has some clear value: it is self-evidently wonderful to find your true love or your lost diary or a hundred dollars in a parking lot. Yet there is also a value to the mere *act* of finding. Some years ago, for instance, I took a detour while driving home, came upon a junk shop I had never seen before, browsed the contents of its single dusty bookshelf, and, for one dollar, purchased a lovely first edition of a volume of poetry, inscribed and grandly signed by its author: Langston Hughes. I doubt I'll ever stumble on something of so much objective value again, but it was not just the literal worth of the discovery that made it thrilling. If I had purchased the Hughes from a rare-books dealer, I would own the exact same thing but have very different feelings about it, and not only because I would have spent so much more money to acquire it. What made finding the book remarkable was not just what it was but where it was—tucked away among boxes of fishing tackle and cans of Rust-Oleum and stacks of empty picture frames—plus the unlikely fact that I happened to be there, too.

You can take away all the intrinsic value of a find and this intrinsic value of finding will still remain. At that same junk shop, I later acquired a little cast iron whale, perhaps five inches long, which set me back twenty-five cents and which I cherish just for its pleasing heft and the satisfaction of having salvaged it from the world's flotsam. And I am not alone. After the need to economize, that satisfaction is the main reason so many millions of people visit junk shops and yard sales in the first place: because finding even relatively worthless things is reliably fun.

It is so much fun, in fact, that it is one of the primary ways we entertain children. There's nothing inherently valuable about a North Dakota license plate; it acquires its value when, six days and forty-nine other states into a road trip, your ten-year-old finally spots one. This same logic applies to Hide-and-Seek, Capture the Flag, Where's Waldo?, word scrambles, and the countless other games that offer their players no reward whatsoever beyond the pleasure of finding. And it also applies, in its purest form, to coins and four-leaf clovers, which we teach children to treasure and regard as talismanic. Although such things have almost no worth of their own, we consider them lucky, for the circular reason that we are lucky to find them.

This feeling of good fortune forms the essence of almost every experience of finding—even though, as I said earlier, that experience is otherwise highly variable. Sometimes it is an act of recovery. Sometimes it is an act of discovery. Sometimes it looks a lot like learning. And sometimes it just looks like growing up, since much of life's meaning comes from things that, as we get older, we must track down on our own: friends, happiness, purpose, our vocation, our soulmate, ourselves. Still, at its core, finding something always resembles that moment, dear to the heart of six-year-olds, of spotting a penny on the ground: you are the one standing there looking when the world shifts just so and some bright glimmer—a knickknack at the junk shop, the first shining edge of a brilliant idea, the woman you will marry—catches your eye.

LIKE COINS AND four-leaf clovers, falling stars function as a kind of lucky charm; that's why we wish on them. But that habit is a pale version of a robust tradition. Throughout most of human history, meteorites, dimly understood but already recognized as remarkable, enjoyed a status bordering on sacred. A thousand years before the onset of the Iron Age, ancient Egyptians found that metal in meteorites, grasped its provenance (there is a hieroglyph meaning "iron from the sky"), and began using it for ceremonial purposes, including to make the dagger that was buried with Tutankhamun in his tomb. The early Greeks kept a holy stone, long since vanished but widely believed to have been a meteorite, in the Temple of Artemis at Ephesus. Another one, reputed to have fallen from the sky in the days of Adam and Eve, has been lodged in a wall of the Grand Mosque in Mecca for fifteen hundred years. Visitors to a Shinto shrine in Nogata, Japan, have been paying respects to a meteorite there since it fell on the temple grounds in 861 A.D. And for centuries if not millennia before they were forced off their land, the Clackamas people of Willamette, Oregon, regarded a thirty-thousand-pound meteorite as a gift from the heavens, and used the water that gathered in its hollows to cleanse and heal themselves and anoint their arrows before battle.

For a long time, the origins of these strange stones remained a mystery. Some people, unwilling for scientific or theological reasons to believe that fragments of the universe could be dislodged and fall down, insisted that meteorites came from the earth. (Those skeptics included Thomas Jefferson, who once argued that, although it might be hard to explain how else a meteorite landed in Connecticut, it would be considerably harder "to explain how it got into the clouds from whence it was supposed to have fallen.") Others believed that meteorites came from space but disagreed about exactly which part. Only in the twentieth century did the mystery resolve itself. We now know that while some meteorites come from the moon or Mars and a few probably come from comets, the vast majority of them—on the order of 99.8 percent—originate over a hundred million miles away, in the asteroid belt: a kind of vast circumstellar junkyard, filled with the shattered remains of protoplanets that formed some four and a half billion years ago, in the infancy of our solar system.

Every once in a while, one of those bits of debris gets nudged out of its orbit, typically by a collision with another asteroid or by the gravitational influence of Mars or Jupiter, and begins heading toward the earth. For seven hundred, a thousand, two thousand years, it carries onward in its strange new course, loosed from order, a wild streak in the cosmic tidiness. Once it enters our atmosphere, at speeds of up to a hundred and sixty thousand miles per hour, its surface begins to vaporize from friction, leaving a trail of incandescent gas streaming behind it—the shooting part of a shooting star. By the time it has reached the lower atmosphere, much of its original mass has burned away and the fireball has extinguished itself, turning a previously flamboyant object into a plain dark rock plunging toward earth. Unless it is enormous, it will not set anything ablaze when it lands, or, for that matter, bear any obvious signs of its fiery journey. So efficiently does its surface melt away in transit that its core typically remains as cold as outer space. As a result, if you ever happen to be near a meteorite when it falls, you can pick it up right away without fear of being burned.

But that is advice you will almost certainly never need. To say that Billy was lucky to find what he did is to understate the matter dramatically: a meteorite falls on any given square mile of the earth roughly once every twenty thousand years. In all likelihood, the last time one landed anywhere near where his did, the cornfields he knew were roamed by mastodons.

That seems like a lesson in the rarity of falling stars, but it is really a lesson in the immensity of our planet. Some forty-two thousand meteorites strike the earth every year (more, if you count those that weigh under ten grams), but virtually all of them land undetected, somewhere on the ninety-seven percent of it that is either covered by water or sparsely populated. Scarcely more than a hundredth of one percent—perhaps five or six per year—are observed while falling and promptly recovered. The odds of finding one that way, as Billy did, hover around one in a billion.

It would be a shame, then, to lose it again: I will have more to say later about what became of that meteorite, and what became of the boy who found it. But in the meantime, it is worth saying a thing or two about *how* he found it, and about that problem more generally—about how, given the immensity of the earth and our own comparative tininess, any of us ever find anything.

Broadly speaking, there are two ways to find something: by looking or by luck. Sometimes our discoveries happen so purely by chance that it almost seems as if *they* found *us,* careening out of nowhere into our lives. Thus have people stumbled on tyrannosaurus bones in southern Alberta, a lost Caravaggio painting in a French farmhouse, a first edition of *Leaves of Grass* in the gardening section of a used bookstore. Other times, we find things because we deliberately went looking for them, searching square foot by square foot the fields of the world. The ruins of Troy, the polio vaccine, our distant relatives in rural Estonia: such things aren't found without serious and ongoing effort.

These two means of finding—by searching or by serendipity—are not mutually exclusive. Only by great good fortune did Billy happen to be present when a meteorite plummeted to earth; only by spending hours walking the land was he able to find it. That experience is representative of many discoveries. Although it sounds paradoxical, we must often search extensively for something we first came upon by chance. In 1974, for instance, several farmers digging a well in the Chinese province of Shaanxi accidentally unearthed something remarkable: fragments of a clay sculpture that had been buried more than two thousand years earlier, as part of the funeral rites for the first emperor of China. That turned out to be one of archaeology's all-time greatest finds, but it has taken half a century and entire generations of scholars and workers to unearth even a fraction of all the rest: the roughly eight thousand life-size soldiers, horses, chariots, and other figures that together make up the Terra-Cotta Army.

As a practical matter, then, looking and luck often operate in tandem. Psychologically, however, they could scarcely

be more different. Finding something that we labored to locate makes us feel that the world is at least partly subject to
our will: that we can exert ourselves to discover something,
and that the discovery itself is a warranted reward for our
work. By contrast, finding something by chance makes us
feel that we are subject to the will of the world. Much as
inexplicable losses make us invoke things like goblins and
wormholes, unexpected finds make us invoke things like
fate, karma, destiny, and God. Curiously, we are most drawn
to explanations like these when our discovery is particularly
astonishing; it is a strange feature of how our minds work
that the more wildly improbable some welcome development is, the more it feels like it was meant to be. Confronted
by a surprising find, we also feel ourselves confronted by the
governing forces of the universe.

As grand as that claim sounds, you have probably felt this
way about your own lucky finds; in my experience, it is almost impossible not to. Many years ago, for instance, at a
time when I was living and working in Costa Rica, a friend
came to visit and spent a week hiking with me in the Osa
Peninsula, a spectacularly wild region of jungles and beaches
and mangrove swamps in the southwestern part of the country. On our first day, the trail led us across a wide brown
river and through a stretch of tangled forest until we emerged
abruptly onto the coastline. It was low tide, and the ocean
had retreated to reveal an uncanny landscape of huge stone
slabs, roughly rectangular and seamed in between by narrow channels of white sand. We took off our backpacks and
left them on the beach and walked out far enough to lie
down next to each other, each on a giant stone of our own.
We lay there talking for an hour or so, until it began to rain,
the drops startling our faces and making dark little cartoon

*ka-pow!*s on the stones. When we stood up, a sheer curtain of storm was headed toward us across the ocean, and so we retrieved our backpacks and hiked onward, and only much later, after the weather had cleared and we found ourselves on another beach, did my friend realize that while we were lying there talking, she had taken off her sunglasses and set them down beside her on the rock, which is where they had remained when we'd made our hurried departure in the rain.

Together, we looked out at the ocean. The tide was on its way back in; enormous green rollers were dashing themselves ecstatically against the shore. Huge overlapping circles of foam came rushing up toward us, bubbled briefly around our feet, and retreated. Beyond them, the Pacific turned deep blue, then a flat sunlit slate that extended as far as we could see. We laughed; so much for the sunglasses. Then, because we had to return to camp that night and our long break on the rocks meant we were dangerously close to missing the tide window, we turned and started back the way we came.

By the time we reached that first beach again, it was unrecognizable. The stones we had sprawled on lay a hundred feet out in the ocean and who knows how far beneath it; the tide was so high that the swells were breaking against the dense understory of the jungle. Our own spirits, by contrast, were ebbing. Hungry and sun-saturated and tired, we were ready to be done with a lovely but very long hike whose final miles now promised to be difficult. We grabbed tree branches to keep our balance as we walked, getting soaked to the waist and smacked by driftwood and coconuts with each incoming wave. I could barely hear over the surf when my friend, who was behind me, said my name, her voice urgent and strange. A head taller than I am, she had seen what I had missed, trapped in a tangle of branches and seaweed. When I turned around, she was wearing her sunglasses, still strung with a strand of kelp from their unlikely journey home.

It doesn't matter, in moments like that, whether you believe that God has blessed you, that fate has smiled on you, or simply that, in a stochastic world, very unlikely odds have broken in your favor. What matters is that you will feel the presence of some force outside yourself—one that, whether or not it is intrinsically benevolent, occasionally and indisputably produces benevolent ends. A pocket of the universe turns inside out and something that has gone missing shakes loose. Poseidon returns a pair of Ray-Bans. That day in Costa Rica, our hunger and exhaustion and general desire to be done vanished as swiftly as the sunglasses appeared, replaced by an entirely different set of emotions. Amazement, gratitude, wonder, awe: the feelings inspired in us by serendipitous finds are the same ones inspired in us by the cosmos as a whole, and for the same reason—because life gave us something splendid that we did not expect, did not ask for, and did not in any particular way deserve.

FINDING SOMETHING BY deliberately searching for it is a different story. Unlike our lucky finds, which involve essentially no effort at all, intentional finds require patience, planning, resources, time, and work. At their triumphant conclusion, they can resemble their serendipitous kin, since no matter how long you look for something, you will generally find it in an instant—and may feel, upon doing so, equally pleased with yourself and with the universe. But right up until then, searching for something is less about the thrill of discovery than about the practical questions of where and how to look.

Answers to those questions abound; good answers, however, are scarce. Plenty of parents, self-help gurus, and psychics will offer to help you find lost stuff, but most of their suggestions are either obvious (retrace your steps; calm down; clean up), suspect (the "eighteen-inch rule," whereby the majority of missing items are supposedly lurking less than two feet from where you first thought they would be), or New Agey ("picture a silvery cord reaching from your chest all the way out to your lost object"). Catholics might suggest that you pray to Saint Anthony, patron saint of lost things, while technophiles urge you to solve your problem through gadgets. In certain narrow cases, this last method will actually work, as you know if you've ever had your girlfriend call your missing cellphone, acquired one of those little Bluetooth-enabled tracking devices that attach to everyday objects, or used the button on your key fob to make your Toyota Camry honk at you.

But these tricks, while helpful, have their limitations. Your phone needs to be on and non-dead; your car needs to be within range; you need to have the foresight to stick a tracking device onto the thing you're going to lose before you've lost it. If those conditions don't apply, or if you are looking for something that was not previously in your possession, such technologies are no more useful than the eighteen-inch rule. If you are really serious about finding something—or, more gravely, if you have lost something really serious—you do not need gadgets or visualization exercises. You need expertise.

This was the realization the U.S. military arrived at during the Second World War, when navy higher-ups, concerned about enemy submarines, began wondering if there was some way to determine where they lurked. To address the problem, they organized the Anti-Submarine Warfare Operations Research Group, perhaps the first entity in history to regard finding missing objects as a math problem. Although the research group was tasked specifically with finding U-boats, it was essentially trying to figure out the best way to locate any entity at all of unknown location. To do so, its members gradually settled on—to borrow the title of the cornerstone work in the field they pioneered—a theory of optimal search.

These days, optimal search is most closely associated with operations research and computer science, and is best known for helping to lay the foundations for recent advances in artificial intelligence. But the original version applied to the physical realm, and although the math at the heart of it has improved over time, it still forms the basis for sophisticated real-world searches, whether for missing persons or Malaysia Airlines Flight 370. The mathematical details are complex, but the gist is simple. At the beginning of any search, you generate as many plausible hypotheses as you can about where your missing object might be. Those hypotheses define your search area, which may be known and contained ("my apartment") or huge and indeterminate ("somewhere in the Indian Ocean"). Then you divide that search area into sectors and assign two different values to each one. The first reflects the likelihood that your lost object is there. The second reflects the likelihood that, if it *is* there, you will find it. Thus, the odds that your missing wallet wound up in the medicine cabinet might be low, but if it did, you have a one hundred percent chance of finding it there. Conversely, satellite data and fuel capacity might indicate that MH370 almost certainly went down in a particular sector of the ocean, but you are nonetheless unlikely to find it if the water there is twenty-six thousand feet deep. Once you have these two numbers, you combine them to determine the odds of finding your missing object in each sector, then use the combined figures to construct a probability map of the entire search area. Only then do you start looking, beginning with the place you are most likely to succeed and moving on to less likely locations.

All this might sound so intuitive as to seem silly. None of us needs the advice of the United States Navy to start searching for a lost item in the place we think we're most likely to find it, and all of us automatically move on to more improbable locations from there. (In a desperate moment, who among us has not checked to see if we somehow put our keys in the refrigerator?) Yet search theory formalizes something important about the process of seeking: looking for anything requires resources, which, because they are finite, need to be allocated with care. Calculating the best way to do so might not matter very much when you are looking for your daughter's backpack, but it matters very much indeed when you are looking for your daughter.

Searches like that are too urgent to leave up to intuition—and, much of the time, they are also too complex. *Theory of Optimal Search* begins by looking at the simplest type of search problem: "finding a stationary target when no false targets are present." But those tidy conditions rarely apply. Maybe instead of a stationary target, you are looking for a raft adrift on the ocean or a lost hiker who, rather than hunkering down and waiting for help, is moving in unknown directions—possibly including back into a sector you've already searched. Or maybe false targets *are* present. Since all of the sensors we use to look for things are imperfect (eyes, ears, radar, sonar, cameras), any of them may mislead us. You think you've finally found your car in the airport parking garage, but it turns out to be someone else's gray Honda Accord; you think you've discovered a sixteenth-century shipwreck, but it turns out to be just an old schooner, scuttled in the 1970s and breaking apart on the ocean floor.

Worse still, it is not just a wrong target that can draw our attention. Sometimes we home in on entirely the wrong search area. Your lost wallet might be lodged beneath the passenger seat of a friend's car, not in your apartment; your lost hiker might have quit an hour into his trip and headed back to town or left the trail and gone for a swim. It is a dispiriting truth about looking for something that we can only know with certainty where it went missing after we find it.

ALL THIS MAKES looking for something sound dry, somewhere between a low-level hassle and a high-level statistics course. But in fact it is often thrilling, at least if the collective creative output of humanity is to be believed: stories about searching for something are among the oldest, most enduring, and most popular tales we tell. The typical object of these quest narratives is something of immense value stashed somewhere unknown or far away. As with the real things we look for, that object may be concrete or abstract, something the hero has lost or something he or she has never seen before: Jason and the Argonauts searched for a golden fleece, Psyche searched for her lover, Harry Potter searched for Horcruxes, and everyone from Galahad to Indiana Jones searched for the Holy Grail.

Like the inventors of children's games, the creators of quest narratives understand the intrinsic pleasure of discovery, and they know that they can convince an audience to stick with them simply by deferring it. Suspense, after all, is not a product of being unaware that something is out there; it's a product of knowing that it *is* out there but not knowing when, where, or how you will find it. As that suggests, a search also has the great virtue of being, all by itself, nine-tenths of a plot. It gives you a goal (trying to find X) and a climax (finding X) and in between it gives you an excuse to explore interesting new terrain. "When you search for a needle in a haystack," one version of the saying goes, "you come to know the haystack."

That is an elegant way of restating a different cliché: it's not about the destination, it's about the journey. In keeping with that philosophical outlook, many quest narratives are chiefly if covertly about the protagonist's emotional or spiritual development. Never mind the ostensible object of the quest, these stories suggest; the real thing we need to find is ourselves. Before he turned his attention to the Valley of Lost Things, Frank Baum made this point explicit by sending the characters in *The Wonderful Wizard of Oz* out to find their heart, their brain, their courage, and—like a long lineage of questing heroes stretching from Dorothy all the way back to Odysseus—their home.

Other quest narratives make this same case by way of a negative example: a protagonist who fails to mature and instead grows dangerously fixated on finding what he seeks. According to *Theory of Optimal Search*, the challenge of looking for something is twofold: "how to search and when to stop." In stories like these, the protagonist fails to stop, even long after the value of the missing object has been eclipsed by the toll the search has taken in time, money, sanity, and lives. Perhaps the finest example of the quest narrative as cautionary tale is *Moby-Dick,* but there are many others as well. In *Treasure Island,* for instance, the titular treasure barely figures at all; the book is really about greed, obsession, naïveté, hubris, and violence. In the end, when the heroes finally find the treasure, they are, as one hears about lottery winners, no different, better, or happier for having done so.

Taken collectively, the moral of these stories is a sound one: be careful what you spend your time looking for. Pick the right thing and you will be rewarded, sometimes beyond your wildest dreams; pick the wrong thing and you may lose more than you find. The good news is that you don't need to make that choice on your own, since figuring out what to seek in life has been a central concern of philosophy for thousands of years. The resulting wisdom is close to unanimous in cautioning us that our happiness does not lie in the pursuit of material things, à la *Treasure Island,* or the pursuit of revenge, à la *Moby-Dick.* Frank Baum came closer when he sent his characters off in search of hearts and brains and courage and homes, not to mention what they found along the way: friends. Such things truly do make our lives different, better, and happier. The difficulty is that they present search problems of their own.

OF ALL THE things that can make finding something difficult—false positives, false negatives, moving targets, incorrect search areas, lack of resources, the vagaries of chance, the general immensity of the world—one of the thorniest is this: sometimes, we don't really know what we're looking for. Maybe you are trying to find the perfect wedding gift for that notorious Friend Who Has Everything. Maybe you are trying to find someone to date in order to someday have a wedding of your own. Maybe you are trying to find a drug that will impede the development of plaque in the brain. In all of these cases, you are looking for something that is wholly new to you and, in some instances, wholly new to the world. How, then, are you supposed to find it?

That's the question the Thessalian statesman Meno posed to Socrates almost twenty-five hundred years ago. The two men are discussing virtue, and when Socrates confesses that he doesn't know what it is, Meno is troubled. "How will you look for it," he asks Socrates, "when you do not know at all what it is?" And "if you should meet with it, how will you know that this is the thing which you did not know?" Taken together, those two questions became known as Meno's paradox: if you don't know what you're looking for, you can't find it, and if you do know what you're looking for, you don't need to search for it. As a result, you should never bother looking for anything, because your search will be either unnecessary or impossible.

As a logical claim, this is nonsense. All throughout history, we have successfully tracked down entities—objects, ideas, places, people—that we had never seen before and, at the start, understood poorly if at all. Moreover, as Socrates pointed out, to imply that searching is futile is to endorse stasis and incuriosity. "I would contend at all costs both in word and deed," he declared, "that we will be better men, braver and less idle, if we believe that one must search for the things one does not know." But if Meno's paradox is absurd as an assertion, as a set of questions it remains important, and largely unanswered. How *do* we search for things when we don't know what they are? And how are we supposed to recognize them if we find them?

Consider a very basic form of this problem: you have forgotten someone's name. Let's say that you are alone and that it is late at night, so that your only option is to search your own memory. You lie there engaged in a strange form of thinking that involves casting around in the broad direction of where the name might lie. Is it Edgar? Evan? Eric? Ian? Nathan? No—but wait: Ethan! Yes: the name you were looking for is Ethan, and the moment it comes to mind, you know it is correct.

The first notable thing about this kind of thinking is that we are able to do it at all. It suggests that losing a name in our mind has at least one thing in common with losing a wallet in our house: somehow, we know that there are more and less likely places to find it, and we conduct our mental searches accordingly—in this case, ignoring the neighborhood of "Richard" and "Robert" and looking in the vicinity of "Ian" and "Nathan." In other words, although there is a gap in our mind where the name should be, that gap is not empty; instead it contains, as William James once observed, "a sort of wraith of the name." That ghostly bit of information helps the mind refine its search, rejecting the wrong answers even though it doesn't yet know the right one: no, it isn't Nathan; no, it wasn't in Chicago; no, it wasn't on the same trip where the dog threw up in the car. Thus a partial answer to Meno's question begins to emerge. Even when we don't know what we're looking for, we do know what we're *not* looking for, and by gradually ruling out, we can gradually close in.

This ability is not limited to our memories. Along with thinking our way back toward what we forgot, we can think our way forward toward what we never knew—toward, even, what no one ever knew. If we couldn't do this, there would be no internal combustion engine, no general theory of relativity, no *Giovanni's Room,* no democracy. As that list suggests, this ability is also not limited to any particular field of inquiry. While William James was busy reflecting on how it feels to try to remember a forgotten name, his brother was reflecting on how it feels to try to write a novel. In the end, Henry James concluded that authors make their way toward new ideas in the same mysterious way as everyone else: "His discoveries are, like those of the navigator, the chemist, the biologist, scarce more than alert recognitions. He comes upon the interesting thing as Columbus came upon the isle of San Salvador, because he had moved in the right direction for it."

This capacity to arrive at new ideas simply by thinking our way in their direction is one of the defining characteristics of our species, yet we don't really know how it works. We do know that it proceeds by some means more sophisticated than trial and error, since we recognize and move in the right direction, not merely in random ones. As with rejecting "David" but lingering on "Nathan," we can somehow sense certain abstract features of a correct answer before we know it, and, as kids playing search games say, we can tell when we are getting colder and when we are getting warmer. We also know, often instantly and absolutely, when we have found what we were seeking. Interestingly, the cues that tell us this are not just intellectual but also emotional: like finding most things, finding an answer is extremely pleasurable. All of us have experienced the low-level version of this, when a lost name or lost fact flashes back to mind, as satisfying and nearly as involuntary as a sneeze, and many of us have had at least one or two genuine eureka moments—"eureka" being Greek for "I have found it." Such discoveries are like the meteorite in the pasture: a sudden and dazzling appearance, only in the fields of our own mind.

As with everything else we find, we can arrive at these new thoughts slowly or suddenly. Many epiphanies occur after countless hours spent in thought, but others *precede* an extended period of thinking: with ideas as with terra-cotta warriors, we sometimes need to look for what we have already found. Carl Friedrich Gauss once discovered the so-lution to a difficult math problem long before he could prove it was right. "I have had my results for a long time," he sup-posedly said of that experience, "but I do not yet know how I am to arrive at them." Many other scientists and mathe-maticians, from Barbara McClintock to Albert Einstein, have likewise reported finding answers through sudden flashes of insight that then took weeks, months, or years to verify.

This is the kind of experience that baffled Meno. How can we think something that we have never thought before and know it to be true? Socrates had an answer: we can't. He believed that during these seeming epiphanies, we are really just rediscovering things we already knew, not in this lifetime but before it. "As the soul is immortal, has been born often and has seen all things here and in the under-world," he wrote, "there is nothing which it has not learned; so it is in no way surprising that it can recollect the things it knew before." To Socrates, every apparent instance of thinking something novel or finding something new is really just an act of remembering.

This is a beautiful idea, one that explains Meno's paradox in the most evocative of terms. Because we have already seen everything there is to see, bits of it sometimes come back to us like cosmic déjà vu: in the gaps of the mind, a wraith of all creation. As an explanation, however, it is compelling only if you share Socrates's belief that the soul is immortal and capable of retaining memories—and if you aren't bothered by the insult to the mind, which, in this account, can't generate new ideas. What's more, as a practical guide to finding things, this lovely story is useless. Although it claims to explain after the fact how we were able to discover something seemingly novel, it cannot tell us beforehand how to do so.

In fairness to Socrates, though, no other account to date has fully explained this ability either, let alone helped us improve it. That's a pity, because of all the things we look for, the most elusive entities are also the most important. We seek in the darkness not just for a forgotten name but for many of the most fundamental and fulfilling parts of life. "How, then, do I look for you, O Lord?" Augustine asks in his *Confessions,* troubled by the question of where to find God and—as a recent convert to Christianity who had once ardently espoused a different faith—how to know when he has found the right one. And we might echo his question about any number of crucial things. How, then, do we look for a calling? How do we look for meaning? How do we look for friends, a community, a home? How do we look for someone to love? Should we go out in search of these missing aspects of our lives? Or must we simply wait until, by fate or chance or design, they finally materialize on their own?

LONG BEFORE HE found his falling star, Billy understood something about what it was like to plummet unexpectedly into a new world. Given up by his biological parents soon after he was born, he had been adopted and raised, like a child in a fairy tale, by a poor but loving couple who had no children of their own: he was, as we used to say, a foundling. His adoptive parents—forever after, to him, simply his parents—worked in a local cannery, saving up their money in coffee cans to try to buy a farm. When a fire tore through the shantytown where they lived and the cans and their contents burned up, they started over. By the time they had set aside enough to purchase a home, they were getting on in years, and they started thinking about how nice it would be to have some help around the place and someone to pass it on to after they were gone. Thus it was that Billy came along.

America, at the time, was reveling in its modernity. Elvis was on the radio, television sets were taking over the living room, and thousands of brand-new Thunderbirds were about to hit the road. But Billy rode to town as his father's father would have done, in a horse-drawn wagon, and the house he shared with his parents had no indoor plumbing. He did not much feel the lack, scarcity and poverty being common all around him. Whatever was happening in the rest of the country, he grew up in a place where a man asked to indicate his profession might answer "rabbit hunter," and a boy might miss a month of school in harvest season to help out on the farm.

Billy was one such boy, but he didn't mind the disruption. A middling student who seldom enjoyed his classes, he was happier out in the fields than in a schoolroom anyway. Still, he had an uncommon mind—quick to grasp a problem and patient while solving it—and he learned everything his parents taught him with alacrity. His father was fair, demanding, taciturn, and exceptionally hardworking—the kind of rough-hewn, reserved, practical type Wallace Stegner once called "a man with the bark on." His mother was softer, and doted on her sweet-tempered, late-in-life son. Billy, who turned out as he was raised—honest, grateful, good-humored, unafraid of hard work—buried them both before he turned twenty-five.

By then, he could build or fix almost anything, like his father before him; but, also like his father, he had known from early on that he wanted to farm. He made a go of it, but for his generation, it was virtually impossible to survive with fewer than two hundred acres, plus equipment that could easily run to tens of thousands of dollars. For Bill, as he was known by then, it was miles out of reach. He sold his parents' farmhouse and found work at the local A&P, first as a cashier, then as a clerk in the dairy department. Time passed, faster than it once had done. One day while he was working at the store, a young woman came in to do her shopping. He asked around, and the bread-delivery man said he knew her; she was a local girl by the name of Sandy, one of seven children of a mother widowed young. Bill said that, in exchange for her phone number, the bread man could be best man at their wedding. By the end of their first date, she had turned that other gift from the universe into the second-best thing he had ever found. Six months later, at the little church she had attended in childhood, he married her.

Like his parents, Bill was frugal. No matter how little he

made or how much he did without, he had never stopped saving money, and no matter where he lived or what kind of work he did, he had never stopped missing the family home. After the wedding, he bought it back, but by then, the farmhouse had succumbed to termites; he wept the day he decided that he had to tear it down. But one winter morning after a blizzard blew through, he and his new wife lay down outside and made snow angels to mark the place where they would build a log cabin for themselves and the children they hoped to have. Not long after, they broke ground. Before work in the mornings, after work in the evenings, on weekends, on holidays: for three years they labored at it, hauling away two thousand wheelbarrow loads of dirt to dig out the foundation, notching and chiseling and placing each one of hundreds of logs, mortaring the gaps, nailing down the shingles, framing the rooms, raising the chimney, placing hearthstones for the two woodstoves that would keep the whole place warm. Friends and family helped lay the footer and hoist the roof beams, but for the most part they built it themselves, by hand.

When it was finished, the cabin sat in a large clearing, bordered by a stand of trees with a seasonal creek running through it. Inside, in addition to the main room, there was a kitchen, a bathroom, two bedrooms downstairs and a third in the loft up top, plus a room off the back to stack the firewood. Outside the door lay forty acres—his father's fields, his mother's milk house, the long lane down which he had once driven crops to town by horse and wagon. He had come home, finally, and so had something else. The things we find, we find to be lucky: he put the meteorite in the kitchen, on the hearth beside the woodstove, twenty-five years and a few hundred yards from where he found it.

How ARE WE supposed to find love? For me, as for many people, this felt like a fraught question when I was single. Love is not like a lost object, after all: we can't locate it by retracing our steps or thoroughly searching our surroundings. But it is also not like the solution to a problem; we may think about it for a very long time, we may imagine it in vivid detail, but we will never find it inside our own mind. It *is* something like a missing person—in fact, it is quite literally a missing person—but the search area in which we must look for it is essentially unbounded. It could be waiting at the local coffee shop, or three states away, or on staff at a hospital in Senegal, or at a holiday party you're not very enthusiastic about attending, forty cold, rainy blocks from home. To make matters worse, in the majority of cases, it was last seen, by you, never.

This is the kind of predicament Meno would have recognized: how are we supposed to find someone we haven't met and don't know anything about? Love, before we encounter it, is like an idea we've never had before. We may try to fumble our way toward it, but its eventual manifestation is a mystery. This is one of its many delights: love often takes us by surprise, in when and where it shows up and, above all, in who embodies it. But, from the perspective of those who are still searching for romance, it is also a serious problem. Although love is one of the most wonderful things any of us can ever hope to find in life, there is no obvious way to look for it.

Some people, accordingly, believe we shouldn't even try. For reasons philosophical, practical, or tactical, they hold that actively searching for a partner is pointless—that it makes us seem desperate, that love is never where we go looking for it anyway, that it is most likely to appear when we are happy and fulfilled and busy living life on our own terms. Others believe that finding love, like achieving any other goal, requires effort and rewards dedication: that you should "put yourself out there," that you should "say yes to everything," that, by the law of large numbers, enough bad dates—false targets, as it were—will eventually produce a sublime one.

I have spent most of my life in the camp that regards love as, basically, a meteorite—something that comes to us suddenly and out of nowhere; something that we find, when and if we do, by sheer luck. I don't mean to say that I believe in this model of finding love to the exclusion of all others, but I know why I prefer it. For one thing, it reflects a fundamental truth about love, which is that it is out of our control. There are few things in life harder to explain than why we fall for this person and not that one, and few things harder to alter by sheer force of will. For another, it means that there is no reason to organize one's life around the pursuit of love and, therefore, no reason *not* to organize it around work or friends or travel or volunteering or whatever else you choose to do with your time—an expansive, autonomous, fulfilling vision of life for which I am grateful, not least because it has historically been denied to women.

Finally, and perhaps most saliently, I myself have only ever found love by pure chance. At one point, single and well into my thirties, it occurred to me that the things that made me happy in the short term—holing up at home reading, heading out alone on long trail runs, vanishing into the quiet of my work—were never going to lead me to the things I wanted in the long term: a partner, children, a home full of people I loved. That was a sobering realization. By that stage of my life, the solitude I cherished was already shading more and more often into loneliness, and with increasing frequency I found myself warding off sadness about not having a family of my own. Now, for the first time, I felt real fear that I would never find one.

And so, breaking with my own lifelong habit, I began actively looking for romance, recruiting friends and family to the cause and testing the waters of online dating. The former were sympathetic and took my request seriously, but they were also useless. One of them eventually told me, wisely, that my closest friends would never help me find a partner; if they knew that person, they would have already introduced us. Love lurked in more distant circles, an asteroid that needed to be nudged out of its orbit; she suggested that I enlist the help of new friends, friends of friends, colleagues, casual acquaintances—excellent advice that I didn't have the heart to follow. My extremely short-lived foray into online dating, meanwhile, produced results laughably far afield of love. In its mixture of comedy, futility, and awkwardness, the experience was like getting halfway into a pair of jeans in a dressing room and realizing that they are wildly too large or small. It did not take long to give up and revert to my former habit of stifling my sadness and ignoring the problem.

But I am hardly a statistically significant sample, and I have watched those around me find love in all kinds of ways: by searching for it; despite searching for it elsewhere; despite not searching for it at all. I have one friend who responded to a breakup by going on fifty first dates, and another who responded by moving home to be near her family and focus on them and on work. Both are now happily married. I know people who quash with steely finality any attempt to help them find love, and others who mobilize an entire search party to scour the landscape for a likely partner. And I know people who search for love as I briefly tried to do, and as we search for so many things these days: online, via any of the countless companies that have proliferated for that purpose.

How those companies themselves generate matches is its own mystery, since the algorithms they use are proprietary. One way or another, though, they codify what is obvious about looking for love: to turn up a potential mate, we must somehow narrow the search area, impose upon the giant pool of possibilities some restrictions with respect to geography or physiology or taste in TV shows or preferences about household pets. One difficulty with doing so, as almost anyone who has ever tried online dating can tell you, is that no matter how numerous and specific such constraints may be, they will still screen in plenty of terrible matches. But the more serious problem is the opposite one: those same constraints, the ones that we ourselves select, may screen out someone perfect—because, in matters of love, we have no real idea of what we are looking for. Or, rather, we have a great many ideas, any of which may be wrong.

This is a problem, because it is surprisingly difficult to recognize something when we have a mistaken idea of it in our head. We know this from everyday experience, as when we scan our shelves for a book and fail to find it because we are picturing an orange cover when in fact it is blue. In much the same fashion, we sometimes initially overlook our future partner. One of the great tropes of falling in love—in books, in movies, in life—is that we failed to notice it even though it was right there in front of us. We may have known the person, even for years, but barely registered her existence; we may have been good friends, even best friends, yet never considered the possibility of anything more. We may even have felt passionately about the right person but in the wrong direction, as Elizabeth Bennet, in *Pride and Prejudice,* initially despised Mr. Darcy.

The quest for romance, in other words, raises Meno's second question as well as his first—not just how to look for love, but how to know when we have found it. The answer doesn't seem particularly mysterious when two people are already acquainted; over time, they get to know each other better and come to feel that they belong together. In such cases, love emerges, like a photograph, from exposure. But in other, stranger cases, it materializes more like the flash. Of all the enigmatic things about love (its origins, its purpose, the strange and dictatorial selection process over which we, its subjects, have so little say), perhaps the most baffling one is this: sometimes, we seem to know right away that we have found it—even if it turns out to be nothing like what we were looking for, even if we weren't really looking for it at all.

WE MET ON Main Street. C. had driven two hundred and fifty miles to get there, although not to see me; she was on her way from her home in Maryland to a week in Vermont, followed by a wedding in upstate New York, and the town where I lived made a convenient stopping point. A few months earlier, a mutual friend had introduced us by email and, meaning nothing much by it, told us that we would adore each other. We'd exchanged polite notes, and later that spring, while planning her road trip, she realized she would be passing nearby. She suggested lunch; I named a local café. When the appointed time came, I walked to town, ducked my head in the door to make sure she hadn't already arrived, then stepped outside again to wait.

This was in the middle of May, on a day that had dawned chilly but was rapidly turning beautiful. In front of me, the street wound down toward the Hudson River; behind me, the summit of an eastern spur of the Appalachian Mountains was just starting to leaf over into a pale springtime green. That morning, I had gone for a run up there, on a trail that tracked upward alongside a stream until it reached a rocky peak with a view west across the river to the Catskills and south almost all the way to Manhattan. I had moved away from New York City nearly ten years earlier, which meant that, to my considerable surprise, I had now lived in this town with its backdrop of hills longer than anywhere else since childhood. That's what I had been thinking about—the pleasing but also somewhat arbitrary nature of my home—during my run. I don't remember what I was thinking about standing there on Main Street before I looked up and saw C. walking toward me.

It is strange, all these years later, to summon that version of her and that version of me. In Plato's *Symposium*, Aristophanes imagined lovers as two halves of one being, separated by the gods and unable to feel whole until they found their missing counterpart, but C. and I were perfectly whole before we met. In fact, what strikes me now, when I remember that moment, is precisely her wholeness: there she was walking toward me in all of her remarkable specificity, and there I was, still knowing nothing at all about her. Slender, fair-skinned, dark hair falling past her shoulders, improbably dressed for her road trip in an oxford shirt and jacket: that was the sum total of the available information about what had just become, although I didn't know it yet, my new life. In retrospect, I'm not even sure how I knew she was the person I was supposed to meet for lunch, so entirely was she a stranger to me at that moment. Rotate history a billionth of a degree and she would have remained that way forever. Instead, I watched her make her way toward me up the street, closing the last brief stretch of all the space and time before we met.

It is not precisely correct to say that I knew right away. What I felt most of all, over that first lunch, was extremely alert. She was serious-minded and extraordinarily intelligent, so much so that my heightened attention was akin to that of a climber in steep terrain: the peaks high and varied, the views vast and lovely and surprising. She somehow conveyed the impression of being both forthright and reserved, so that when she first laughed, with swift and genuine delight, I instantly wanted to make her do so again. I watched her as she talked, her long fingers organizing the air between us as precisely as a conductor; I watched her movements, formal yet easy, as the day warmed and she took off her jacket and cuffed her sleeves. We sat and talked in the empty outdoor patio of the café for two and a half hours, although it felt like half that—or, really, felt loosened from the forward hurrying of things altogether, as if Old Man Time had caught a glimpse of us and temporarily waived the rules, like the kindly airport cop who, laughing, let us linger over a long farewell in a No Stopping Zone outside Departures some weeks later.

Finally, after we had finished a last superfluous cup of coffee and returned our dishes to the counter inside, I obeyed an impulse that remained opaque to me and invited her to come see my place before she got back on the road. We walked there together and I showed her the little carriage house where I lived and the garden out front, the tomatoes and peppers still no higher than our ankles, the bean plants just starting to unfurl like tiny periscopes from the earth. Then, suddenly uncertain why I had brought her there or what to do next, I wished her safe travels, and we bade each other a slightly awkward goodbye. When I went back inside, I was startled to realize how late it was in the day.

That evening, she wrote to me: "I'm woefully out of practice at this sort of thing and you live three states away, but I'd love to take you to dinner next time we're anywhere near the same city." Two things happened so fast that I'm not sure I'd even gotten to the end of that sentence before my brain began its life-altering reorganization. First, as with an optical illusion where one image suddenly resolves into another, the afternoon we had just spent together entirely rearranged itself. It had not crossed my mind, before getting that note, that C. dated women—which is why, I suppose, I hadn't correctly registered the nature of my own intense focus on her. Second, I knew without thinking about it that I was going to say yes.

We went on our first date a week later, when C. was on her way back from her friend's wedding. After dinner and a movie that we both thought was terrible, we headed out for an evening stroll. I can still remember the exact route we took, and also the wending way we walked, now closer and now farther, the shifting amount of space between us suddenly uppermost in my mind. The night was mild and cloudless. A crescent moon chaperoned us from its usual discreet distance, vanishing and reappearing among chimneys and treetops. Occasionally that laugh of hers rose into the air, like starlings startled from their roost. By the time we got back home and settled into my couch, I was intensely aware of how much I wanted to touch her, and also how much I wanted to keep sitting there listening to her. It is my fault, then, that it was so very long past midnight when we finally kissed.

I will not try to describe it, except to say that I could; I mean that it is one of those rare moments, out of only a handful each of us gets in a lifetime, that remains imperishable in all its particulars. We had, by then, strayed outside again. The moon had set. Stars and quiet filled the sky. All around us, the universe was expanding, not from something, not into anything, all on its own, changing the scale of space, stretching the boundaries of existence. Gravity, electromagnetism, the strong and the weak, all the known and unknown forces were exerting themselves on the cosmos. If we felt them, if we ever feel them, we did not know it, brimming as we were with our own forces, spinning inside it all like the tiniest of Ptolemy's heavenly spheres. Afterward, I led her back indoors. For a long time after that, everything that wasn't her—the house around us, the rest of the world, the passage of time, the past and the future—retreated into unimportance.

The next morning we woke up shy and happy and amazed, in ways both large and small. How little we still knew of each other: she was startled by the tattoo on my shoulder, which she hadn't noticed in the dark; I was startled to find that her serious brown eyes had turned a lovely sunlit green. Hazel, she acknowledged, but I thought, *magic*, and I have thought of her as magic-eyed ever since. We left the house together, choosing to walk to town for coffee rather than make it at home, and on the way up the little hill outside my front door I took her hand in mine. It was different, thrillingly so, from how we had touched the night before, more chaste yet also more definitive. Overnight, I had become someone who wanted to hold someone's hand on the way to breakfast.

She left by noon, although not before surreptitiously pulling a volume of poetry from my shelves and leaving it, opened to a perfectly chosen page, where I was sure to find it. When I did, a few hours later, something in me flared upward, like a candle newly lit. If I hadn't already known before that moment, I knew it then.

WHEN DANTE ALIGHIERI was nine years old—but really almost ten, he notes, summoning a child's attention to fine gradations of time—he happened to notice, in his hometown of Florence, a girl about his own age. Her name, he learned, was Beatrice: grantor of blessings. Much later, in *La Vita Nuova,* he described, in strikingly technical terms, what happened at the instant he saw her: "the vital spirit that resides in the lofty chambers of the skull to which all the nerves report spoke in its astonishment to my eyes, saying: 'Now has your bliss appeared.' "

Of all the great passions recorded in Western literature, the one of Dante for Beatrice is among the strangest. Unrequited, unconsummated, and almost entirely ungrounded, it seems, at first, less like a model for enduring love than like the prototype of a hopeless crush. Nine years after that initial encounter, they meet once again—whereupon, to Dante's infinite joy, Beatrice greets him. After that, they pass each other in the street from time to time, but they never exchange another word. Then, when Beatrice is just twenty-five, she abruptly dies.

It is a tragedy unpreceded by a romance, unless you take seriously the possibility of falling in love at first sight. But Dante did take it seriously. He declared Beatrice to be the perfect woman, credited her with his own spiritual improvement, and dedicated dozens of poems to her, not to mention his entire life, past, present, and future. And yet, aside from her good standing in the community, he knew virtually nothing about her—nothing of her turn of mind, nothing of her preoccupations and dreams, nothing of the topography or temperature of her inner world. There was, in short, nothing that could have given rise to his love for her, except for the instantaneous response of his "vital spirit."

It is easy to dismiss as ludicrous the notion that anyone could find love this way. To its many detractors, the idea of love at first sight is at best foolish, at worst dangerous, and either way utterly fantastical—a gauzy, outdated fiction sustained into modernity by Hollywood screenwriters, hack novelists, and hopeless romantics. According to these critics, what we think of as a profound emotional experience is instead a shallow response to mere physical beauty—for what else could so capture our attention in the first few moments of meeting someone? Likewise, what we think of as a sign that we have found the right person is nothing of the sort. We would be less impressed by couples who plunge precipitously into love, they argue, if we consistently tracked the outcome. Plenty of relationships begin quickly and with passionate conviction only to fizzle just as fast; others end years or decades later, after those who fell rapidly in love fall gradually out of it. We do not know the answer to the alternate-universe question that *La Vita Nuova* tempts us to ask: would Dante and Beatrice have been happy together?

This skeptical outlook is a useful corrective to a long-standing fairy-tale vision of love, which, in addition to excluding all kinds of people from the ranks of possible lover and beloved, also excludes most of what is required for serious, sustained, grown-up relationships. "We are daily bombarded with messages that tell us love is about mystery, about that which cannot be known," the scholar and activist bell hooks wrote in *All About Love*. "We see movies in which people are represented as being in love who never talk with one another, who fall into bed without ever discussing their bodies, their sexual needs, their likes and dislikes. Indeed, the message received from the mass media is that knowledge makes love less compelling." Yet in reality, hooks argues, knowledge—a deep, intimate, sometimes hard-won understanding of both one's partner and oneself—is "an essential element of love."

I agree entirely with all of this. And yet, indisputably, love *is* mysterious, and one of its many mysteries is that we do sometimes know very early that, as Dante put it, our bliss has appeared. "At first sight" might be an overstatement, but quibbling with the idiom is beside the point. Regardless of the exact duration of a fleeting exposure—a first glance, a first interaction, a first conversation, a first date—we can sometimes recognize, incredibly quickly, that we have found our beloved. The moment he saw her in the grocery store, Bill, that grown-up finder of a falling star, knew that he had met his future wife. My mother asked my father to marry her on their second date. For them, as for many people, love appeared as suddenly and as obviously as an idea coming to mind. *Eureka:* I have found him; I have found her.

But what is it that we are registering when this happens? Despite what the critics say, it can't simply be physical beauty. We have all admired the look of a stranger for whom we feel nothing else, which means that we are perfectly capable of being instantly drawn to someone's appearance without being instantly drawn to them more generally. When the latter happens, then, we must be responding to something more than their surface features. You could argue that this "something more" is just an unusually intense degree of attraction, but that restates the problem rather than solving it: what is it that we perceive, in this one person over and above even other very attractive people, that we find so compelling? And, just as puzzling, how do we do so? Through what as-yet-unfathomed part of ourselves can we obtain enough information about someone to conclude so quickly that we are meant to be together?

People have been trying to answer these questions for a very long time. Consistent with his overall account of knowledge, Plato believed that we can identify our beloved by memory. For him, there was no such thing as love at first sight; there was only love that we recognize because we saw it once before, long ago, before our own lifetime began. (Some couples genuinely experience their connection this way, feeling, from early on, as if they have known each other forever.) Setting aside all the other questions this theory raises, it does have the virtue of offering a plausible mechanism for how people fall in love so rapidly. A glancing interaction with a stranger can teach us only so much, but we know from experience that a recollection, however faint or fleeting, can instantly summon powerful emotions.

Many of Plato's contemporaries, however, had a different explanation for how we fall in love at first sight. In Roman as in Greek mythology, passion was often depicted as imposed from the outside, by Cupid or Eros, who used their bows and arrows to send love winging through the air as swiftly as a glance. As monotheism came to dominate the West, gods and their weapons gave way to sorcerers and mischief-makers, often armed with potions—some of them applied, in keeping with the idea of love at first sight, directly to the eyes, as Oberon and Puck do to Demetrius, Titania, and Lysander in *A Midsummer Night's Dream*. Across the centuries, a great many other thinkers and writers, from Boccaccio to Yeats, agreed that passion was generally delivered this way—that, as the latter wrote, "love comes in at the eye." Dante, however, disagreed. In his telling, the eyes are the last to know; they recognize the beloved only when the "vital spirit" alerts them.

Of all these explanations, the mythological one is the most evocative, simultaneously elevating and mocking our mortal intimacies: love feels sometimes like a private miracle, sometimes like a lowercase act of god. In terms of metaphorical richness, I am not sure that account can be bested, even if we have to scrub the tarnish of familiarity off the arrows to remember how golden they are, and how pointed. But it was Dante who made falling in love at first sight seem modern. To explain it, he turned not to our past life but to our current one, and not outward to the gods but inward to the brain, the body, and the psyche—all the places we now routinely look to try to make sense of ourselves. Together, those various parts form a kind of distributed information-processing apparatus whose conclusions, he tells us, are only belatedly made available to his conscious awareness.

Dante's apparatus is, of course, the human mind, that remarkable machine for making sense of ourselves and the world. We still know only marginally more about it than he did, but what we do know suggests that we should not be altogether surprised by how quickly we can recognize that we have found our beloved. One of the hallmarks of human cognition is the ability to draw sweeping conclusions from limited data, often with incredible speed. Thus do we respond to a sharp sound combined with a sudden shift in the light by leaping away from a falling tree branch; thus do we understand from our sister's two-syllable greeting on the phone that she is calling with bad news; thus do we walk into a room full of strangers and know from the looks on a dozen unfamiliar faces that something is extraordinarily wrong. Why, then, should we not meet someone new and infer just as swiftly—from a glance, a conversation, a lunch—that we are safe, that there is good news, that something is extraordinarily right?

The naysayers, unappeased, will still doubt our ability to feel so much for a near stranger. Yet that is a miserly take on our human capacities, and one that is inconsistently applied. Not all sudden love is equally suspect, after all; no one questions the overwhelming love parents feel for their children the moment they are born. I don't mean to suggest that loving an infant and falling in love with an adult are analogous experiences—only that deep mutual understanding cannot be the sole grounds for feeling an overpowering connection to another person. And not all sudden knowledge is equally suspect, either. Countless words have been written in praise of hunches and gut instincts, and while such intuitions can easily lead us astray, even the most conservative epistemologist will grant that on occasion, in ways that can't all be dismissed as coincidence, they are spectacularly correct. Although we can't yet explain how we do it, we do sometimes come into many kinds of knowledge almost instantly.

When that knowledge is the knowledge of love, it can change our lives not only with incredible speed but with incredible thoroughness. This is the thing I try to explain to people who are still looking for a partner and despair of ever finding one: not having found love and finding love are wholly incommensurable conditions, yet you can cross from one to the other in a single day. Dante did, the instant he met Beatrice—an experience he later described with perfect concision and, although he normally wrote in Italian, in Latin, to give it its due gravity. *Incipit vita nova,* he wrote, of the moment of finding love: a new life begins.

I WAS NERVOUS BEFORE our second date. It seemed entirely possible that C.'s interest in me would have waned by then; it also seemed entirely possible that the exhilaration I had felt on our first date—a wild happiness amplified by the anticipation of more happiness—would evaporate when we saw each other again. At the time, I had a reputation among my friends as being impossibly stubborn about romance. I had dated plenty, but generally briefly; not since college had I been serious about anyone. In my twenties, that was normal enough, especially once I moved to New York. But by my mid-thirties, when more and more people around me had found a partner and settled down, my persistent failure to fall in love had come to seem like a problem. One friend, assessing my tendency to identify within days all the reasons a relationship wouldn't work out, described my heart as optimized for detecting red flags. Another joked that I was waiting around for the sudden appearance of a female Prince Charming.

Of the two accusations, the latter was closer to the mark. Although it's true that I could always come up with a reason why someone I'd dated wasn't right for me, it was never actually *the* reason. The real reason, in every case, wasn't the presence of something that made me think *no;* it was the absence of anything that made me think *yes.* I had tried, exactly once, to make a relationship work without that strong inner sense of assent—partly because I was trying to take seriously the theory that my romantic pickiness was a means of avoiding the vulnerability inherent in love; partly because it seemed possible that the feeling of certainty could emerge over time rather than being present from the beginning; and partly because that particular relationship seemed, on paper, as if it should work. But it did not, and the effort to pretend that it someday might was uncomfortable for me and terribly unfair to the other person. After we broke up, I promised myself that I would never make that mistake again. Later, when I met C. and the sense of *yes* rose up in me unbidden, I felt intense relief that I had been right about myself, and right to wait. But hope never materializes anywhere without fear having stowed away inside it, and in the time before our second date, I worried about feeling so much based on so little, and dreaded the possibility that those feelings would evaporate when I saw her again.

And then there she was, one sunny Friday afternoon, standing in my doorway with a bouquet of flowers in her hand. Many years later, she would give me a book by the literary critic Philip Fisher about the feeling of wonder—about, among other things, how we respond to rare and remarkable sights, from rainbows to great works of art to a drop of water under a microscope. In it, he notes that at the moment of suddenly comprehending something new ("the moment of getting it"), people almost always smile. That day, seeing C. in my house again, I smiled and couldn't stop smiling. What I understood then was that no amount of happiness was out of proportion to the fact of having found her. I took the flowers and set them on the table and stepped into the place in her arms where they had been, and there among the wild clamor of things I felt were two almost contradictory emotions: that nothing in the world could feel more natural; that nothing in the world could feel more astonishing.

Never mind the obvious candidates, things like passion and adoration and anxiety and bliss; the characteristic emotion of falling in love is amazement. The experience is, above all, one of being astounded by what lay in store for you. "I can't believe you're real," lovers say to one another in complete sincerity, as if the beloved were a gryphon or an angel. In many other contexts, a sudden confrontation with the unpredictability of the world leaves us sobered or distraught—as when loss shocks us with how abruptly something we cherish can disappear. But falling in love is the shining flip side of that encounter, an instance of the deep joy we can feel when life surprises us.

Surprises work by revealing what was previously obscured, teaching us something while also, in many cases, exposing how little we know. All throughout that second date with C., I kept thinking about a pair of lines by John Keats: "Then felt I like some watcher of the skies / When a new planet swims into his ken." My understanding of the universe rearranged itself when I met C. Almost right away, I recognized that I now knew one of the most important things in life—the person with whom I wanted to share it—while simultaneously recognizing that I knew almost nothing at all about her. That kind of ignorance, unlike many other kinds, isn't invisible or passive. It is obvious and urgent, and it actively seeks its own eradication: to no small extent, falling in love is a state of yearning for information. If, like Dante, your feelings are unrequited, you will try to glean every last detail you can from afar. If you are luckier, you will make a comprehensive and intimate study of your beloved—of her body, her mind, her heart, her habits, her home, her everything. In its thoroughness and avidity, this thirst for knowledge is representative. In general, any longing in love—physical, emotional, intellectual, existential—is always the longing for more.

And that, I suppose, is why my second date with C. lasted nineteen days. We hadn't planned to simply keep spending more and more time together, of course. But she had come north again in part because she had a series of meetings that month in New York City, and I lived an easy train ride away from Manhattan. It was late spring in the Hudson Valley. The cherry and crab apple trees down the lane were still a riot of pink and white, the stores on Main Street had their doors propped open, the season of farmers' markets and strawberry festivals and outdoor music was just beginning. Stay, I suggested, and she did.

Incipit vita nova: in the days that followed, we moved through life together in whatever is the opposite of a haze, vivid and alert, as if we were not only new to each other but new to the world. Once, early on, we strolled through a park and along a creek until we reached the Hudson River, the afternoon light filling its thousands of blue pockets with silver and gold. Look, C. said every few minutes as we walked south alongside it, pointing out the shadow of a bluefish darting beneath a rock, a toad half-buried in the mud, a heron standing stock-still on the bank. When she was little, she told me, she had been interested in indigenous civilizations, so her father had spent hours out walking fields and shorelines with her, helping her learn to recognize pottery shards and axe-heads and mortars and arrowheads. At ten, she spent an entire summer in a makeshift archaeological dig her parents set up for her behind their house; at twelve, on a visit to the beach, she searched around in the sand and found a grateful stranger's missing wedding ring. Maybe it was that early training that sharpened her focus, or maybe she is just naturally attentive to the world; at any rate, I soon learned that she notices everything. At a walking pace, she can spot a four-leaf clover in the grass and a praying mantis on a leaf and a clutch of eggs in a nest in the crook of a tree. Even when she is driving, which she loves to do, she points out turtles on the riverbank and hawks on the tree branches and a fox trotting daintily away across a distant field, all without ever seeming to take her eyes off the road.

That is how all of life with C. felt to me from the beginning: unusually detailed, unusually distinct. I loved to be in the world with her, to look at it alongside her and see what she saw. One day we went strolling around Storm King, that beautifully named mountain with its equally beautiful outdoor sculpture garden, getting slightly sunburned under a sky that was perfectly cloudless—the word, C. told me, that Nabokov used to describe his fifty-two-year marriage to Véra Slonim. Another day we wandered through a local contemporary art museum, which, because its exhibitions included towering stone megaliths and crumpled cars and piles of shattered glass, I jokingly described as the Museum of Fear-Based Art. I see your point, C. said, standing at my side, looking up at a nine-foot-tall spider by Louise Bourgeois; then she told me about the folk artist James Hampton's *Throne of the Third Heaven,* with its injunction to "FEAR NOT." Later, back at home, we sprawled together on the couch, watching *Double Indemnity* and devouring an entire pizza, indolent and satisfied as house cats. The next week we rambled together up and down the back roads of the Hudson Valley, crisscrossing creeks and admiring old farmhouses and talking about the kind of home we dreamed of someday having; and when, back at the car, she turned and stretched and smiled at me, lithe and sunlit with the first smattering of summer freckles on her cheeks, I thought about Pablo Neruda, who gave us the sweetest filthy lines of poetry ever written. "I want / to do with you what spring does with the cherry trees": I wanted that with C., too, but of course I did. The number of things I wanted to do with her was infinite.

Poor Dante; he found love, but he never got to learn that love is also its own ongoing kind of finding. The thrill of that first moment of recognition replicates itself again and again in the early days of love, like the single gold coin glinting up from the seafloor that leads to all the varied and immeasurable treasure of a Spanish galleon. Every one of those early days with C. felt like that, filled with new discoveries—some deep and arriving in the form of deliberate disclosure, some ordinary and gleaned from mere proximity, from being beside each other while life carried on. I learned, over the course of that extended second date, that C. takes her coffee black and all day long; that she dislikes talking on the phone but regularly drops handwritten letters in the mail by the dozen; that she is close to though strikingly different from her two sisters, one of them two years older, the other six years younger; that she wakes up fully rested after five hours of sleep; that she has no sweet tooth whatsoever but much the same relationship to salt as those grand wild creatures, elephants and buffaloes and mountain goats, which will cross rivers and mountain ranges to satisfy their need for it. For her part, C. learned that I love to travel but am prone to motion sickness; that I prefer to sleep in a room as dark as a medieval village on a moonless night; that I cannot tolerate music before ten in the morning; that no matter how miserable the weather or how tired I am or how soon we have to be somewhere else, the right answer to "Should I go for a run?" is always "Yes."

Love, like grief, has the properties of a fluid: it flows everywhere, fills any container, saturates everything. Even the most quotidian activities of that second date were flooded with it. I loved going grocery shopping with C., loved doing the dishes with her, loved being near her while doing my usual day's work. Like me, C. is a writer; during that long second date, she mostly worked at my dining room table, surrounded by books and files, while I wrote nearby at a standing desk, which she took one laughing look at and promptly began referring to as my unicycle. On days when we needed a change of scene, I took her to a public library I liked a few towns to the south, where we sat in a little study with green-shaded lamps and grand oil portraits and armchairs that looked as if they were designed for wolfhounds to sleep beneath them. When that space was occupied, we laid claim instead to a wide wooden table in an airy atrium, where rabbits and robins had forty meals a day in the grass outside and I got distracted watching her face in the afternoon light, angled and serious with thought. Eventually I

showed her, for the first time, a draft of a piece I was strug-
gling to finish, and she showed me the opening pages of the
book she was just then starting to write.

Often when we weren't writing we were reading, sometimes for work and sometimes for pleasure, sometimes together and sometimes separately. One day she pulled James
Galvin's *The Meadow* off my shelves and took it to the
couch and finished it in one sitting—or not a sitting, really,
since she lay there on her stomach, heels kicked up behind
her like a bookish kid on a rainy Sunday, too absorbed in the
novel to notice how often I looked up from my work to take
her in. At night, we read aloud to each other, from whatever
book we were each midway through or from something we
loved and wanted to share, as when I confessed that I hadn't
read much Frank O'Hara and she took a volume of his poetry up to bed. "When I am feeling depressed and anxious
sullen / all you have to do is take your clothes off," she began,
her voice low and intimate and amused, and made an instant convert out of me.

This, then, was my new life; it was almost impossible to
believe. I was amazed—daily, hourly amazed—that something so wonderful had happened to me. I will retain forever
one particularly acute version of this feeling, which seized
me sometime in the course of that long second date, when I
found myself in the kitchen at three in the morning, making
pancakes. We had come downstairs from the bedroom after
C., who has the figure of a sylph but, as I had discovered by
then, the metabolism of a sixteen-year-old boy, announced
that she was famished. Now she was perched on a stool,
plate on her lap, serenely devouring her eighth or ninth pan-
cake. A jar of jam sat open on the counter. The faint bakery

smell of flour and butter filled the air. Outside the window, the whole scene floated in duplicate, golden in the darkness. My happiness was so enormous that it was like an entire third person standing there beside us.

I had lived, up to that point, an extraordinarily fortunate life. Safety, prosperity, good health, an excellent education, a job I adored, a loving upbringing that had left me at peace with myself and at ease in the world: all of life's least equitably distributed goods had been mine to enjoy. My portion of suffering—an acquaintance with grief that began too early, the everyday sorrows and fears no one alive can avoid—was modest by any standard, my portion of joy immense. So it was shocking, when I met C., to feel it grow so swiftly and so much. That "watcher of the skies" Keats wrote about was William Herschel, the astronomer who, in identifying Uranus, increased the known boundaries of the solar system by nine hundred million miles almost overnight. Thus did my happiness expand when I met C.

The morning after those predawn pancakes, I woke to an empty bed. When I went downstairs, I saw C. through the big front windows of my house, sitting at the picnic table out on the patio, long since settled into work. She was wearing jeans and a plaid shirt rolled up at the sleeves; there was a cup of coffee at her side and a legal pad in front of her. Her back was to me, and I stood and watched her through the window for a very long time. The night before, in the kitchen, the world with her in it had seemed enchanted— seemed, in its shimmering, small-hour joy, almost unreal. But what I could not stop looking at that morning was the utter ordinariness of the scene: there she was, going about her life in my home, going about her life in my life. The next day, when she went into Manhattan for work, I called my sister and told her that I had met the woman I was going to marry.

THE STORY OF romantic love, the poet Anne Carson once observed, is always a story about the lover, the beloved, and the differences between them. That is true. But it is also true that the story of romantic love, especially as the lovers themselves tell it, is always a story about the lover, the beloved, and the *similarities* between them. Both contrast and likeness are inevitable in love, and our culture is conflicted about which matters more. Folk wisdom tells us that opposites attract, while also telling us the opposite of that. "You simply must meet So-and-so," the would-be matchmaker insists. "You have so much in common."

What do C. and I have in common? The strange thing about the list I could make is how difficult it is to say which items on it contribute substantially to our happiness and which are insignificant. The first time I got in her car, she started the ignition and Miranda Lambert came blasting out of the radio, because she had left the local country music station turned up to eleven. She was embarrassed, but I was elated, somewhat irrationally. It's true that I love country music, and also that this preference is shared by relatively few of my friends (and disparaged by plenty of them), but I don't know why catching her in the act of loving it too should have moved me so much, or felt so promising. In the scheme of things, does anything matter less?

Yes, actually, and we have plenty of those things in common, too: a fondness for thrift stores, a lifetime supply of flannel shirts, a distaste for that alarming pseudo-vegetable known as baby corn. All of this is small-bore stuff, obviously. It has nothing to do with our beliefs about love and commitment, child-rearing and families, ethics and politics, the nature of the self and the origins of the universe. Yet much of life is lived on the small-bore scale, so who's to say that such things matter less than the deeper visions and values we share? When couples at their weddings celebrate a mutual love of something that seems, at best, peripheral to an enduring partnership—Dungeons & Dragons or bacon or cosplay or the films of Wim Wenders—it is not simply because that thing helped draw them together but because, to them, it feels laden with significance. Even or perhaps especially in its seeming triviality, it is a kind of shibboleth: proof of their rightness for each other, a manifestation of the astonishing improbability of ever finding one's own bespoke and perfect love. Perhaps that is why, in my experience, you will seldom find a happy couple that does not take pleasure in some seemingly shallow thing they have in common.

Still, even if you and your partner are similar in ways both superficial and deep, you are assuredly not *that* similar. "Resemblance does not make things so much alike as difference makes them unlike," Montaigne observed. "Nature has committed herself to make nothing separate that was not different." And C. and I are, in certain respects, extremely different. Some of those differences I discovered over time, but others I recognized from the beginning. During our first lunch, when I did not yet understand why I was tracking her biography so attentively, I registered, with the same heightened interest I brought to everything else that day, a host of obvious gaps between us: of age, of background, of geography, of religion.

Of these, the last was initially the most striking. On my mother's side as well as my father's, I am Jewish—or anyway, as the old joke goes, Jew-ish. When I was young, my parents took my sister and me to synagogue on the High Holy Days, hosted a Seder every Passover, filled all eight days of Chanukah with delight, and saw to it that we celebrated a few other kid-friendly holidays throughout the year, too—Purim, Sukkot, Simchat Torah, Tu B'shvat. I attended seven years of Saturday school (though it was held on Sundays, presumably to avoid competing with field hockey and soccer practice; our temple was so suburban that it was actually *called* Suburban Temple), and when the time came, I learned a Torah portion and summarily became a Bat Mitzvah.

For some children, all this would have been sufficient to nurture a life of faith. But ours was not a great synagogue, and I was not its greatest student; I completed my ostensible religious education with only a superficial grasp of Jewish history, very little in the way of theology, and nothing at all that could be called faith. Just about the only thing it fostered in me was the sense of being connected to something very old and very fragile, and a love of the traditions that constitute that connection. I still light candles on the Jewish holidays, in the name of my ancestors and out of respect for the notion that each of us is obliged to help dispel the darkness in the world; I am still moved to joy by the Shehecheyanu, that rising prayer of gratitude reserved for special occasions; I am still rendered solemn by the recitation of the Kol Nidre on the Day of Atonement; and very few things can return me to the expansive wonder of my childhood as swiftly as a fragment of Hebrew scripture or the keening beauty of a Hebrew song. The ancient call of the shofar, which lingers in a sanctuary so long after it is sounded, has likewise lingered in me.

But my religiosity, such as it is, ends there. Questions about goodness and justice, suffering and evil, the origins and ends of the universe, the nature of the self, how to treat one another, how best to live our brief lives while we have them: all these are of passionate interest to me, but I have never found satisfaction or solace in any faith-based answers to them. By constitution, education, or both, I am profoundly skeptical of religious authority, and although I am deeply interested in the many fathomless mysteries of the universe, I do not believe that an omnipotent creator numbers among them.

C. does. From her earliest childhood, she has felt that, as the poet Gerard Manley Hopkins put it, "the world is charged with the grandeur of God"; to her, holiness has always been manifest in everything. She grew up in the Lutheran church, studied theology after college, and, for a time, contemplated joining the clergy. Eventually she turned to writing instead, but not before working for a while as a hospital chaplain and in parish ministry. When we met, she was still occasionally preaching on Sunday mornings, if the local pastor was ill or out of town, and presiding, upon request, at weddings and funerals.

This was not the kind of difference between us that could go unremarked, even in our earliest days. My own religious background and irreligious convictions were hardly subtle, and the first time we spent a Saturday night together, C. got up the next morning and went to church. My initial and in some ways most enduring reaction to this—not to her faith but to my falling for someone so devout—was to regard it as a grand cosmic joke. I once had a thoroughly brilliant editor confess to me, after I had waxed enthusiastic about the International Space Station, that he wasn't particularly interested in anything above the level of the stratosphere. Before C., I had been in relationships with people who, figuratively speaking, felt that same way: fascinated by all kinds of worldly matters but largely indifferent to many of the cosmological and existential questions that I care about most. Such adventures in dating were generally doomed on those grounds alone, but not in my wildest imagination did I expect to remedy the problem by falling in love with someone whose first and most abiding relationship in life is with Jesus.

Still, comic or not, I wasn't naïve enough to imagine that this double difference—the gap not only between her Christianity and my Judaism but between her faith and my atheism—wouldn't matter. There were practical issues, for one thing. I wasn't sure that I could have a Christmas tree in my home, and I wanted our hypothetical future children to feel at least partly Jewish, and to be better educated about what that meant than I had been. (Our kids, apparently, would go to Saturday *and* Sunday school.) And there were potential emotional issues as well. I am still sometimes aware of a kind of happiness I can't bring to C., the kind she might find with someone who went to church with her every Sunday, bowed their head in prayer with her, and stood together with her under the shelter of a shared faith.

But C. assures me that she herself neither imagines this kind of happiness nor mourns its absence, and it is true that I have never sensed in her any longing for me to be other than who I am. Nor do I have any desire to draw her convictions closer to my own; I find them moving, illuminating, and inseparable from who she is, and I would not change them if I could. Still, they remain foreign to me, and sometimes it shows. Unlike C., who has always taken my Judaism and atheism seriously and finds both of them morally compelling, I cannot claim to be consistently charitable about Christianity. Once, when she told me that in her childhood church she had served as both a crucifer (carrying the cross into and out of the sanctuary) and an acolyte (lighting the candles at the altar), I responded with the smart-aleck observation that the latter figure should really be called a lucifer.

She laughed then, just as she has laughed every time I have teased or blasphemed or expressed bemusement about her faith. To the best of my memory, our different cosmologies have never caused either of us any real friction or fear—partly because they are each too robust to require the other's obeisance or participation but chiefly because, as different as they are, they are not actually all that incompatible. The difficult lesson I learned in my previous relationships was that there is a limit to how close you can get to people who do not care about the same questions you do, not through any failure on their part but simply because their minds orient along different meridians than yours. Conversely, the wonderful lesson I learned from falling in love with C. is that if you do care about the same questions, it doesn't necessarily matter if you arrive at the same answers. C. and I did not, but our minds turn naturally toward the same things—to the problem of origins and endings and the enigma of how to live meaningfully in between. She points them out in all their endless daily variations to me, like hawks in a tree or herons in the reeds, and I can't imagine ever needing more than that: to be at her side in the vast fields of mystery.

———

NONE OF US knew it, of course, but my father had eighteen months left to live when I fell in love with C. I wish he had been with us for five or ten or twenty more years, but I am grateful every day that he lived long enough for the two of them to meet. I told him and my mother about her some-time during that marathon second date, and not long after that, while planning a quick weekend trip home to Ohio to see them, I realized that I very much wanted her to come with me. It was early in a relationship to propose such a thing, and shockingly early in the context of my own past behavior; but I knew that my father was in poor health, and I knew, already, how serious I was about C. I asked my par-ents what they thought about meeting her and they were enthusiastic, and I asked C. what she thought and she said she would be honored, and that is how, one week later, the two of us found ourselves on the side of the road in the middle of nowhere, waiting for a tow truck.

The middle of nowhere was, in this case, central Pennsyl-vania. We had left the Hudson Valley on a Friday afternoon, talked until two hundred miles of highway had unfurled be-hind us and darkness filled the car, then found a nearby place to spend the night. The next morning, we got up, got breakfast, and, twenty minutes down the road, got a flat tire. I had neither a spare nor any form of roadside assis-tance (in point of fact, I didn't even have a car; for compli-cated reasons, I was driving my parents' own car back to them), but C. had a Triple-A membership, so she called and requested a tow. Then she fetched our iced coffees from the front seat, led me to a shady patch of dandelion-strewn grass, and sat me down beside her to wait.

Meanwhile, three hundred miles to the west, there was a photo frame hanging in my parents' upstairs hallway. Procured by my mother sometime in the distant past, it was the kind designed to hold one school picture for every year from kindergarten through twelfth grade—designed, that is, to humiliate those of us who endured a ten-year awkward phase. I had never had the heart to ask my mom to take it down, but, although it couldn't have occupied more than a square foot on the wall, when C. and I got in the car that morning to resume our drive, it was occupying something like thirty percent of my brain. Even in elementary school, when children as a rule are still adorable, I was an aesthetic calamity, and it only got worse from there. In addition to baby fat, braces, and curly hair that I had no idea how to handle, I had absolutely no fashion sense and no desire to acquire one. Instead, I delegated the matter to my well-intentioned but old-fashioned mother, with the result that I showed up at school every day for years looking like a miniature middle-aged woman.

As an adult, I am mostly amused by and in many ways grateful for my socially oblivious childhood, so I was surprised to feel a flush of real embarrassment when I imagined C. looking at those photos. I understood, intellectually, that all of us have things in our past that make us cringe, and that real intimacy requires sharing them sooner or later. But she and I were still very much on the side of sooner, and I briefly wondered, there on the Pennsylvania Turnpike, if I could somehow slip away for a moment shortly after we arrived and mortification-proof my childhood home.

But that was impossible, of course. The pictures were hardly the only things troubling me, and the rest could not be hastily removed while C. was off chatting with my parents. There was the bedroom down the hall, still full of its childhood detritus (open the wrong cabinet and a jumble of Breyer horses, Billy Joel CDs, and marching band paraphernalia was liable to come crashing down on top on you); there was the house itself, which was large even for a family of four and unreasonably gigantic with just my parents living in it; and, least avoidable of all, there was the ritzy sweeping-lawns-and-Tudor-mansions town where it was located. The suburb of Cleveland where I was raised was a good place to grow up but also—as I have thought for as long as I have thought about such things—a good place to leave. The most accurate thing I can say about my feelings for my hometown is that they are mixed: somehow, it is simultaneously such a fundamental part of myself that I can't imagine being me without it, yet so very unlike me that I can't imagine ever choosing to live there.

That morning, driving west with C., I couldn't stop picturing it through her eyes. It brought home, so to speak, another kind of difference between us, one that was as obvious as religion but had not clamored so urgently for my attention until we were headed straight toward it. C. grew up four hundred–odd miles and many cultural time zones from me, on the Eastern Shore of Maryland—that stranded little piece of the state that is part of the Delmarva Peninsula, bounded to the west by the Chesapeake Bay and to the east by the Atlantic Ocean. Until 1952, when the Bay Bridge was built, it took several hours to reach the mainland from her future hometown, with the result that the area developed like an island: slowly, distinctively, in relative isolation. In the decades since then, it has largely retained that early character, making it as culturally distant from as it is physically close to the Northeast Corridor.

Part of that cultural distance stems from its political geography. The northern border of Maryland lies flush with the Mason-Dixon Line, and life on the Eastern Shore, unlike in Bethesda or Baltimore, remains distinctly southern. It was the Shore that gave us those great patriots Frederick Douglass and Harriet Tubman, while also giving us the men and women who enslaved them. The failure of Reconstruction to reconcile those parties and redress those wrongs lingers in the region, as in so much of the nation, in the form of persistent racial injustice, widespread de facto segregation, and scattered Confederate flags. But other and better southern influences linger on the Shore as well: in the instinct for hospitality; in the August-afternoon pace of life; in a population made up about equally of the congenitally reticent and natural raconteurs; in the elaborately preserved and frequently recited communal genealogies whereby So-and-so's granddaddy worked with Great-uncle Jack on your mother's side at that mechanic shop out on Hog Barn Road back before your Aunt Lula was born. The South or some part of it also lingers in the accent in which all this gets recounted, which sounds like the city of Pittsburgh sold off its consonants to the Carolinas. Whenever C. is around her family, she lapses back into it, and every time, it makes me want to kiss her.

Traditionally, most people on the Eastern Shore have made their living off the land or the water, but the construction of the Bay Bridge brought with it wealthy retirees and commuters seeking second homes on the water. Still, outside of a few small cities and some pockets of extraordinary affluence, the area remains largely rural and working-class. When I was growing up, my friends' parents were doctors and psychologists, lawyers and business professors and petroleum engineers. The adults around C. were truck drivers and construction workers, farmers and watermen, welders and waitresses. Like ninety-five percent of the people in her hometown, neither of her parents went to college. Her mother worked as a mail carrier for the United States Postal Service and spent her free time helping C.'s father, who, to support the family, held down three or four jobs at a time: cleaning a bank, stocking a store, hauling trash, scrapping metal, landscaping and caretaking for the owners of those second homes.

The town where C. was born and raised is not, technically speaking, a town—just a census-designated area, consisting, according to that census, of one hundred and sixty-seven families, including hers. In keeping with the dual identity of the Shore, she grew up on a farm and could drive a tractor before she drove a car, but she spent her childhood picking crabs and begging uncles and family friends to take her fishing. She also spent her childhood working alongside her parents—sorting scrap, stacking firewood, helping empty the trash and vacuum the carpets when they cleaned the bank. On her own time she attended 4-H in the evening and vacation bible school in the summer and was shocked, once she left home, to learn that New York City was only four hours away. In short, for all intents and purposes, C. was from the working-class small-town South, while I was from the moneyed Midwest—the heartland not of farmers and autoworkers but of oil magnates and railroad barons— which is the contrast that was on my mind when all of a sudden in the middle of Pennsylvania the tire went flat.

All of falling in love is a kind of hiatus, a pause in the normal order of things. Workaholics in love start knocking off at five, early birds in love linger in bed until noon, cynics

in love turn their starry eyes upon the world and declare it
beautiful. But that morning by the highway was something
else, a kind of pause within the pause—a little lacuna, of a
piece with our first lunch, into which we slipped while time
looked discreetly away. There was nothing in the world to do
but sit there beside each other and wait. We were not in a
pretty place. I imagine, although memory does not supply
it, that there must have been trash along the shoulder of the
road and the smell of diesel fuel in the air and the intermittent hot windy rush of a tractor-trailer in the near lane. But
all of that, if it existed, didn't matter. What mattered is that,
somehow, as we sat there talking, my sense of looming exposure began to diminish, and the conviction deepened
within me that I had found someone who, if I could stay by
her side, would make life better no matter what was happening to me or to us or to the world.

We were still so new, so young in relationship terms; we
had so much left to learn about each other, so much to work
out, so much to decide. Yet there by the side of the highway,
time seemed for a moment as it really is: the past long gone,
the future unreal, the present perfectly sufficient. On the
phone, the tow guy had said ninety minutes, give or take.
Two hours had passed. The ice in our coffee had melted.
The shade had vanished. In the bright midday light, our
jeans had turned pleasingly warm and the dandelions looked
like children's drawings of the sun, round and rayed and
brilliantly yellow. It seemed possible, and not at all troubling, that we might continue to sit there next to each other
forever. Well, C. joked, looking out at the road in front of us
with its ongoing lack of tow trucks, maybe it's true: you
can't go home again.

I laughed out loud. Of course! What had I been thinking,

driving westward so full of worry about what C. would make of where I was from? Most of us fit only partially into our past selves, and most of us are only somewhat at home in our former homes. Even if we love them, even if we sometimes long for them, even if we know them down to the last ancient orange spatula in the kitchen utensil drawer, we inevitably outgrow them; the world is so big that anywhere you're from eventually becomes parochial by comparison. It's not just that once you leave your hometown behind, you encounter very different people and places from those you first knew. It is that your own past life starts to look different as well. In that sense, the self-consciousness I felt about my childhood home was really (as it so often is) something closer to other-consciousness—an awareness of how a place so familiar to me would look to someone who had never been there before.

But it was foolish, I realized in that moment, to worry about that with C., who knew far more than I did about how it feels to fit incompletely into your own life. Even as a young child, she had had an unusual, serious, famished mind, and—partly because of that, and partly for reasons she could not quite name, even to herself, until much later— she had always stood slightly apart from other people. When she learned early that she liked to read, her mother began bringing hand-me-down books home from the customers on her postal route; her father, who didn't share her literary bent, supported it the best way he knew how, by building shelves for her in the bedroom she shared with her younger sister. When she discovered that she also liked to think, she cultivated the ability to do so regardless of her surroundings, a habit that meant she sometimes unnerved those around her with her quiet. In school, her unapologetic focus on academics would have earned another kind of kid (me, for starters) a reputation as a nerd. Instead, she had the implacable cool of someone who is always slightly keeping her distance.

At seventeen, she went off to Harvard, on a scholarship that didn't cover textbooks or trips home or meeting a class-mate at a café instead of the cafeteria. She got a job cleaning the dormitory bathrooms and, in her first semester, spent a total of twenty-three dollars. In many ways she was at odds with the culture around her, but in one crucial respect, she was not: for the first time in her life, she found herself in a place where the educational offerings matched her desire to learn. She studied English, ran the literary magazine, made friends with graduate students and professors and the head pastor of Memorial Church. She spent evenings in the li-braries, reading and thinking, while her peers assumed she was at cooler parties than they were. After graduation, she went to Oxford on a Rhodes Scholarship and used the extra money from the stipend to travel all over Europe and the Middle East. Finally, ten years after she left home, two years before we met, and some uncountable number of cultural light-years from who she had been when she left, she moved back to the Eastern Shore.

By then, she lived, like so many people who venture far from their roots, in two largely non-intersecting worlds. Certain core parts of herself were invisible or inexplicable to most of the people she had grown up with; others were opaque or alien to those she met as an adult. She generally handled that bifurcation with ease, but all of us yearn to be seen in our fullness, and never more so than when we fall in love. We yearn for it so much, in fact, that we fear it—or, rather, we fear that if we *are* seen in our fullness, we will no longer be loved. That's what I was worried about in the car on the way to my childhood home: that once C. and I got there, she would see in me the vestiges of my awkward younger self, together with all the banality, insularity, elitism, and entitlement associated, sometimes rightly, with the suburbs. Only later did I learn that she had a mirror image set of fears. Never mind the exceptional résumé, the encyclopedic mind, the fact that she can clarify the finer points of Hegelian philosophy and quote Marianne Moore: C. still worried that, when I saw her against the backdrop of her past, she would seem like just some windblown hayseed who had, as they say in the place where she grew up, gotten above her raising. To this day, in vulnerable moments, she worries that she will somehow reveal herself, to me or to the world, as a rube.

Nothing is more ridiculous to me, for all kinds of reasons: because she is brilliant and cosmopolitan (including in that beautiful root sense of the word: a citizen of the cosmos); because I love her country origins; because, as she knows better than anyone, the assumptions about rural and working-class life on which her fears rest do meager justice to the reality. Yet at the same time nothing is more understandable to me. No matter where you come from, no matter how proud you are of your family, no matter how much or how little you differ from the person you love, it is very difficult, in the face of intense scrutiny, to never for a moment be embarrassed by who you are.

Eventually, inevitably, couples lead largely overlapping lives. Over time, you start to share more and more things: your friends, your families, a home, a morning routine, a favorite restaurant, an annoying neighbor, that winter when the pipes kept freezing, the cat who liked to sleep on top of the refrigerator, the first Christmas, the forty-fifth Seder, that terrible health scare, the time you got a flat tire on the Pennsylvania Turnpike. And yet, even with this steady expansion of common ground, the enduring challenge of every relationship is to love across difference. That remains true no matter how similar you and your beloved might be, or might have become. Love is so often written about analogically—"my luve is like a red, red rose," etc.—yet the point of the beloved, the whole reason that you are in love with her, is that she is like no one else on earth. That includes you: your beloved is not like you.

No one ever makes their peace with this fact immediately, and no one ever makes it just once. We are called on over and over to remember that the person we love does not always have the same thoughts, feelings, frames of reference, reactions, needs, fears, and desires that we do. But overall, the trajectory of a happy relationship, which begins with cherishing similarity, ends in cherishing difference. I could never declare with authority what I love most about C.; I love too much of her too much. But it is not a false consolation or a convenient exaggeration to say that I am most often moved to gratitude and tenderness and awe by those parts of her that are least like me—because it is in them that I see her most clearly, and because it is thanks to them that my own world has grown so much larger. And I *can* declare with authority that her ability to love those parts of me that are least like her is the greatest gift anyone, outside of my parents, has ever given me.

As it happens, C. and I found our favorite expression of this peaceful relationship to difference in one of the things we have in common. One night, when I was feeling anxious about some parting of ways between us that I can no longer recall, she reached into her mental bookshelves and came out with a poem that I, too, had loved for years: Robert Frost's "West-Running Brook," which takes the form of a conversation between two newlyweds. They are out walking, following the course of a stream that runs west, and one of them points out that this is strange, since all the others in the region flow east, to the sea. Nature requires that this one must eventually end up there, too, but:

> It must be the brook
> Can trust itself to go by contraries
> The way I can with you—and you with me.

To go by contraries: that is what C. and I had been doing from the beginning, without the phrase for it, and it is what we promised each other that night we would always do— move through the world together yet each in our own way. I have never found it a difficult promise to keep, chiefly because, like the brook, no matter where I wander in any given moment, I am ultimately compelled in one direction. "'Where is north?' 'North is there,'" the poem begins, but listening to C.'s voice flowing on through the rest of it that night, lovely and shady and sunlit, I thought, as I have thought ever since then: *north is you*.

WE DID, OF course, eventually make it to Ohio. I don't remember much about the remainder of the drive, but I do remember our arrival. My parents—no fools, and no strangers to me—knew what it meant that I was bringing someone home to meet them, and by the time we pulled into the driveway, they were almost as excited about C. as I was. ("We have trimmed the bushes, fixed the leaks in the roof, painted the inside of the garage, brushed our teeth, and made ourselves very huggable," my father had responded when I'd emailed that morning to say we were on our way.) I recall a flurry of introductions in the hallway, my father inquiring with characteristic expansiveness what we needed by way of food and drink, my mother radiantly happy just to have us in her home. Then I walked C. into the living room, settled next to her on the couch, and listened as she fielded a classic Isaac Schulz interrogation.

It wasn't until I was well into adulthood that I realized how many people, when they first met my father, found him terrifically intimidating. Anyone who came into his orbit immediately became the focus of his omnidirectional curiosity and his unbounded instinct for hospitality, which together went flying toward their object in a gust of jokes, questions, rapid-fire information, and heavily accented English. None of this ever fazed me, because I knew from age zero that he was all bluff, benevolence, and adoration, but it scared the living daylights out of some of my shyer friends. In country songs, fathers greet their daughters' suitors by sitting on the front porch saying nothing and polishing a gun. My father would invite you inside, offer you a sandwich, a scotch, three different flavors of ice cream, tell you anything, ask you everything—and, for a certain kind of person, be twice as frightening.

C., as it turned out, was not that kind of person. I have seldom been more filled with joy—and also already something like pride, so thrilled was I to have her in my life— than that first day when I sat there listening to her talk with my parents. (It filled them with similar joy, my mother told me later, to sit there watching us.) Amid all the questions and answers, one exchange in particular stands out, occasioned by the fact that C. was raised, as no one in my childhood was, to say "sir" and "ma'am" to her elders. My mother—who had worked hard to instill good manners in her own children—found this charming; my father wanted to know if her parents had served in the military. No, sir, she explained; she was just from the kind of family, and the kind of place, where that's how things were done. Well, be that as it may, my father said, you're to call me Isaac from now on. I have never known C. to miss a beat, and she didn't miss that one. "Okay, Sir Isaac," she said.

My father laughed, not only out of appreciation but, I think now, out of a kind of recognition. From the beginning, he adored C., and, although the two of them were born two continents and forty years apart, I suspect that he saw in her something of himself. That made him, as usual, swifter than I was: before that day, I hadn't noticed any similarities between the two of them, doubtless because of their far more pronounced differences. In addition to the obvious ones of age, gender, and background, my father was almost always gregarious, while C., when not at home, can sometimes be reserved. But they were both people who came from one context and steered themselves into a very different one by sheer force of intellect, and sitting there listening to them talk, I was struck by how much her mind reminded me of his.

Like my father, C. has the kind of relationship to knowledge that comes from early scarcity—or, maybe more aptly, from late and sudden abundance, from first picking up a newspaper or venturing off to the library and realizing that you could simply choose to sit down and learn. I imagine that some childhood autodidacts feel chronically anxious about the legitimacy of their erudition. But both C. and my father, having learned to think by themselves, somehow managed to carry on thinking *for* themselves: they had deep, serious, original minds, ones far less susceptible than most to the parroted or the glib. They also had, between them, the two most remarkable memories I have ever encountered— memories so rapid, well-supplied, and reliable that they functioned as a kind of accessory intelligence, readily furnishing needed information and supplying, among disparate subjects, subtle and surprising connections.

The flip side of this particular gift is that they were both driven crazy by any brief glitch in their normally near-perfect recall. In the face of one of these, my father would push his glasses onto his forehead, squinch one eye closed, look upward, look pained, produce a long, rolling *aaaaaaaaaaaaaccchhhhhhhhh*—a kind of Semitic "argh," made up of sounds my palate can't even produce—and say, in a tone of dire irritation, "Come *on*, Isaac." C.'s version of this, I have since learned, involves saying, "Gimme a minute" (by which she means "Do not under any circumstances make any noise or say anything at all right now, including 'Never mind'"), then burying her head in her hands and, if she is sitting, curling inward, as if the missing fact is stored somewhere near her knees. Thus have I seen the two of them berate themselves into finally remembering, say, the name of a minor character in a lesser Balzac novel they last read a decade ago—circumstances under which, I should add, I myself would struggle to recollect even the title.

Over time, I would discover other things about C. that reminded me of my father, not all of them on the brilliant-and-charming end of the character spectrum. These include an intermittent but impressive obstinacy; the capacity to intimidate other people, usually although not always by accident; and, in contrast to their overall equilibrium, a short fuse, lit by a kind of flaring pride, in the face of perceived slights. But that day as I sat next to C. on the couch, all those discoveries lay in the future. In the moment, listening to her talk with my father and realizing how similar they were in certain ways, I also realized that this shouldn't surprise me at all—indeed, that it wouldn't surprise even people who had never met my father or C. or me. Because this is another theory about how we find love: we recognize it when we come across it because it is familiar, not from before our lifetimes, as Plato thought, but from our earliest days. If it is true that our relationships with our first caregivers shape the romantic choices we make in adulthood, small wonder that I was drawn to someone so stubborn, self-made, independent, devoted, and brilliant.

Among the other things C. and my father had in common—as I'd known since she postponed a date with me to catch an Orioles game—was a love of sports. The morning after the interrogation on the couch, as the four of us walked up to the entrance of a local diner where we were headed for brunch, she said, matter-of-factly, "There's LeBron James." Sure enough, there he was, emerging enormously from the restaurant next door. This was after he had returned from the Miami Heat and before he left again to join the Lakers, during that long, beautiful run when he transformed the Cavaliers from one of the worst teams in the league to NBA champions, finally ending the half-century-long losing streak of every professional sports team in town. Because C. and I were visiting just for the weekend, and for the momentous reason of introducing her to my parents, it hadn't occurred to me to try to do anything touristy with her—take her to the art museum, say, or the Rock & Roll Hall of Fame. But seeing LeBron that morning was the most Cleveland thing that could possibly happen in Cleveland; it was like heading into a patisserie in Paris and watching the Eiffel Tower walk out.

In the diner, C. and my father commenced kibitzing about sports. He ribbed her for stealing the Cleveland Browns and rebranding them as the Ravens; she countered by simultaneously disavowing any responsibility for franchises in Baltimore ("the Western Shore," as people on the Eastern Shore call the rest of Maryland and people from there do not) and pointing out that, circa 1996, the Browns were not valuable enough for the alleged stealing to count as more than petty theft. Around the edges of all this, we ordered lunch, and when the sandwiches and coleslaw and pickles were distributed and the ketchup requested and the waters and coffees refilled, C. asked my parents how they had met.

I had heard the story countless times, of course. When she was an undergraduate at the University of Michigan, my mother had begun dating a fellow student—as fate would have it, Lee Larson, my father's best friend from back in Detroit. When they were still just kids, Lee and my dad had made a solemn pact that if either of them ever started to get serious about a girl, they would introduce her to the other for approval. Lee was a man of his word, and so, when he found himself captivated by my mother a decade later, he arranged a lunch. Whatever my father might have thought of the match turned out to be irrelevant. By the end of the meal, my mother knew that, of the two men at the table, the one she wanted to marry was the one she had just met.

As a kid, I'd always loved this story, not least because it had the thrilling whiff of scandal about it. (Albeit of the comic, all's-well-that-ends-well variety: "Uncle Lee," as I grew up calling him, found his own wonderful woman to marry, moved to a town thirty minutes from my childhood home, and, as long as my father lived, remained his closest friend.) But sitting with C. across from my parents as they jointly recounted the tale—interrupting, expanding upon, and editing each other's versions—I suddenly registered it very differently, the way I might have if she and I had been having brunch with two friends who had only recently started dating. Out of nowhere, it struck me that my parents had always felt as I did now; for the first time, their history snapped into focus as a love story.

To be clear, I had always known that my mother and father loved each other. It was impossible not to know that; they were open and tender and, in my father's case, sometimes cheerfully risqué in their affection. I even knew that, all those years later, they were still *in* love with each other, one of those lucky couples for whom time had worn away the rougher edges while polishing the core. If anything, my father had grown more expressive about his love over the years, more openly grateful to my mother. She was, I understood, his rock, his comfort, his right hand and heaven knows his left brain, his fashion consultant, his ethics committee, and the most gorgeous woman he'd ever met. And I knew that my father was my mother's sunlight and starlight, her best friend, her all-time best decision, her Library of Alexandria, her occasional pain in the neck, and the chief reason she laughed so much every day. But I had nothing to transpose all that knowledge onto until I met C., no way to imagine how their relationship had felt from the inside.

Now, sitting beside her, looking across at my mother and father, forty-eight years after they first sat down and looked across at each other, I was suddenly, irrationally happy for them.

And for me, too: I was so very lucky, I realized. In another sense as well—this one thanks to both of my parents—I'd recognized love when I'd found it because I had seen it from my earliest days. Without ever having to think about it, I had always known what it would look like: loyal, stable, affectionate, funny, forbearing, enduring. My sister, in adulthood, once put this very beautifully. Our parents, she said, had given us a love of ideas, and also the idea of love.

THE IDEA OF love is one thing; the practice is something else. Consider, for instance, the stupidest fight that C. and I have ever had, which was about whether you are more likely to see a bear while out hiking or out backpacking. It may or may not help to know that we were, in fact, out hiking at the time, in Shenandoah National Park, and that we had, in fact, just seen a bear. It was, as bears are, very obvious, pale of snout and sporting a shaggy Bon Jovi hairstyle and swaying tranquilly through the woods mere yards from the trail. It was also magnificent, the way wild animals spotted in the actual wild always are, and the argument was not its fault.

We didn't begin fighting right away. In the moment, we were busy feeling lucky to be outside on a beautiful day, in a lovely and apparently megafauna-filled forest. We discussed the bear for a while once it had disappeared among the trees—its slightly comic shape, its utter indifference to us, the way it hauled its grandeur around like any mundane thing—and then the conversation, like the trail we were on, looped away. But sometime after that, we began talking again about animal sightings, and I made an offhand comment about how funny it was, after all the backpacking trips in bear country where I had assiduously carried my food in canisters or hung it high up in trees, that I had finally seen a bear up close when we were just out hiking for the day.

There are certain fighting words in relationships: *you always x, you never y, calm down, grow up, I don't have time for this.* Among these you will not find "How funny to see a bear while just out hiking for the day." Likewise, wildlife does not appear on the list of subjects couples fight about most often; those generally run more toward money, sex, romance, kids, in-laws, and chores. But that is because any such list is inherently a little misleading. Although it is true that money and chores and so forth are common causes of domestic friction, a huge number of arguments between couples are triggered by something invisible to outsiders. In fact, that morning on the trail, the inflammatory nature of my remark was, at first, invisible even to me. "Just out hiking for the day," I had said, and C. fell silent, and I knew right away, as one always does in a relationship, that something was wrong.

Every couple fights, of course. Even if you are lucky enough to find a partner who is as committed to your well-being as you are to hers, no one person maintains perfect equilibrium all the time, and no two people glide smoothly along through a life consisting exclusively of tenderness, lust, and contentment. To begin with, you must contend with whatever issues, external as well as internal, you and your partner brought into your relationship when you met. These are all but unlimited in number and variety, although

they often take broadly recognizable forms: health problems, financial worries, unhelpful habits formed in earlier
relationships, the inward toll of how a culture treats its different individuals, and the aftermath of past emotional
trauma. In some cases, that trauma can render the very idea
of love suspect. For those who have experienced love chiefly
as withdrawal or cruelty, who have had it wielded against
them by parents or partners or others and were made to suffer in its name, it can be difficult to believe in a version that
is tender and generous, let alone find it and sustain it. A re-
grettable truth about our species is that our capacity to love
is matched only by our ability to harm and hinder that capacity, and one measure of how fortunate you are with respect to fate, family, and society is how much you have been
left free to find happiness with another person.

Still, even if you have a relatively unimpeded capacity to
love, sooner or later, you or your partner or the two of you
in collusion will find plenty of ways to tax it. C. and I are
lucky in that, however much our upbringings differed in
other respects, we both had the good fortune of growing up
in happy families. Partly because of that, neither of us
struggles to imagine or commit to a loving relationship. And
life is easy on us in other ways as well. We have the same
values around money and are sufficiently well-off that financial stress seldom exerts pressure on our relationship. We
also have the same job, and so, although we go about it very
differently, it is easy to help each other, and to make allow-
ances for the other's schedule, habits, eccentricities, and
work-related bad moods. We both derive pleasure from
cooking and cleaning (so much so that a friend once joked
that by getting together we had deprived two other potential
couples of clean sheets and decent dinners), with the result

that it is almost impossible to imagine quarreling over the laundry or the dishes. But none of this kept us from torpedoing a perfectly lovely hike over a disagreement about a bear.

Like most of our arguments, or anyway most of the memorable ones, this one took place during the first year of our relationship, a time when C. and I fought terribly. I don't mean that we had exceptionally terrible fights (although they certainly felt that way to me in the moment), or that we fought terribly often (we did not). I mean that we were terrible at fighting. As it turns out, all those obvious differences between us that had worried me when we met—of age, geography, class, religion—did not matter nearly as much as one I wasn't even aware of for quite some time. This was a difference of temperament, which manifested, most notably, as two wildly divergent strategies for handling conflict between us.

In the world at large, C. is not one to walk away from a fight. Once, when we were in New York City together, we stepped into a subway car where a man was arguing with a woman—not a little domestic squabble but the kind of loud, profanity-laced, menacing confrontation that seems like it could tip over at any moment into violence. Her instinct was to move toward him to be ready to intervene if necessary; mine was to hustle her to the next car to steer us clear of any possible danger. Her response struck me as scary; mine struck her as useless. As that suggests, C. is not afraid of confrontation. She would never start the physical kind, although she admires the courage of those who place themselves between the vulnerable and the dangerous, but at the verbal kind, she is formidable. It isn't that she is liable to lose her temper. On the contrary, she is liable *not* to lose her temper, or at least not to show it in the usual ways. If anything, conflict makes her cooler, more focused, more exactingly logical. When persuasion is what's called for, she can be stunningly convincing; she once talked some strangers down the street from us into taking down the Confederate flag in front of their home, an act of neighborly diplomacy I was certain would fail. But woe betide anyone who belittles her or underestimates her or provokes her disgust. I have seen her riled like that, and it brings to mind a flag snapping in a thunderstorm.

Curiously, though, in the privacy of our own relationship, C. is not like this at all. In the face of a conflict with me, her instinct is to retreat into herself, to tend to her wounds while thinking her way through and eventually out of her anger or hurt or fear. By contrast, my instinct in the face of the same conflict is to rush toward it—not because I am fearless about confrontation but because I am a peacemaker down to my last nucleotide and can't bear the feeling that something is wrong between us. As a result, in the early days, whenever anything was amiss in our relationship, we were almost comically mismatched. What she needed most in such moments—a little space and time to herself—was the one thing on earth I was least equipped to provide, because what I needed most was to immediately know what was wrong so I could set about trying to fix it. Neither of us was ever any good at getting out of this bind, even after we had been together long enough to understand each other's needs, and even though each of us genuinely wanted to accommodate the other. For me, sitting there tranquilly doing nothing while she vanished was like sitting there tranquilly doing nothing in a nest of yellow jackets. I could not manage it for even a minute, and when I tried, which I did, and thought about her silence and withdrawal, I just got more and more stung.

This was the phase of our relationship we were in during that hike in the Shenandoah Valley, when I made the comment about the bear and she went quiet. Predictably, then, when I asked her what was wrong, she said, "Nothing." Eventually I learned that this response was not meant to shut me out, which was how it felt, so much as to shut herself in, to buy a little time to convince herself that it was true. The same went for "I'm fine" when she was not: I experienced it as a blatant lie (which it was), but she meant it as a relative assessment, a way of persuading herself that whatever was bothering her was either irrational or insignificant in the context of our relationship. And in the context of the world, too: for C., who sometimes struggles to believe that her own emotions matter, "fine" was also a way to cut her problem down to size, to remind herself that she was neither bleeding to death nor succumbing to famine.

Both reactions were consistent with a larger part of C.'s character, which is that she is a genuine stoic. Once, speaking of yellow jackets, she was out gardening and I was inside making lunch when I heard the front door open and close. I went about my business, figuring that she had come inside to use the bathroom, but a few minutes later, when I'd heard nothing more, I hollered amiably from the kitchen to make sure she was okay. "Stay where you are," she said evenly, so of course I did nothing of the sort, which is how I discovered that she had accidentally jammed a shovel into a wasps' nest out under an old tree stump in our yard and was now standing in the bathroom, shaking live ones from her shirt and killing them. She had been stung upward of twenty times and made less noise than the moon when it sets. Had

I not come to check on her, I imagine she would have gone on to treat her stings and change her clothes and sometime later told me that I shouldn't go outside for a while because there were a bunch of wasps flying around. And she would have preferred it that way because, in keeping with her stoicism, she hates to be fussed over. (That's a preference I cheerfully ignore these days, partly because one of the great pleasures of being in love is fussing over your partner and partly because her position is untenably unilateral: she *loves* to fuss over me.)

As someone who gets teary-eyed at rom-coms, analyzes my feelings about my feelings, and shows off my cuts and bruises like a six-year-old, I naturally find stoicism absurd. But the truth is that C. really is good at self-soothing, both physically and emotionally, and if I had been able to leave her in peace for twenty minutes that day on the trail, the whole thing would have blown over like the wispy little cirrus clouds overhead. But I could not, so I goaded her into talking to me, whereupon I learned that what she had heard, in "just out hiking for the day" was dismissiveness—an implication that the activity we were engaged in was a pale version of what I really wanted to be doing.

There was some context for this. In the long solitude of my life before I met C., I had spent as much time as I could in the wilderness. She knew how deeply at peace I was in the backcountry—especially in the mountains, especially out West—and she worried that she had taken me away from something I needed and loved. What I should have done was tell her that I needed and loved *her*, that I treasured the texture of the life we were making together, and anyway that it was not a zero-sum game; the mountains could not take me away from her, but I could take her to the mountains. Instead, confused and hurt by how she could have heard in my idle observation something so cutting and so contrary to how I actually felt, I got defensive and told her that I hadn't meant that at all, that I had meant only exactly what I had said, and that after all it did seem surprising to encounter a bear during a relatively short afternoon hike. The trouble was that this had been a poorly thought-out comment the first time around and did not improve with repetition. You don't need to know anything about the distribution of black bears in Shenandoah to know that, in places full of people who are irresponsible with food, they are perfectly likely to hang out near popular trails. C., who hadn't wanted to talk about her feelings in the first place, was only too happy to take advantage of this logical weakness and argue instead about bears.

This is how couples wind up fighting about idiotic things. I can remember, one summer vacation when I was young, sitting with my sister on the front steps of a little rental cabin in northern Michigan while my parents had an epic fight inside. I was alarmed—a peacemaker even then, it terrified me when they argued—but my sister, three years older and cool-headed enough to understand that the spat in question was not going to end in divorce, was amused. "Do you know what they're fighting about?" she asked, by way of comforting me. I did not. "They're fighting because Dad forgot to get tuna fish at the store," she said. How do people who love each other wind up in a raging fight about tuna fish, I wondered at the time. Now I knew.

It took C. and me over a year to work it out (not the bear; the general problem of how we fought), and the solution did not turn out to be what I thought it would. At first I tried to stop pounding so soon and so loudly on the walls of her privacy when she was upset, and she tried not to leave me alone for too long in the tundra of her retreat. But however important compromises may be in international relations, they seldom work well in personal ones, especially not for differences that run deep; you can't build a long, happy life together by abandoning or altering core parts of yourself. Instead, what ultimately changed was not something within us but something between us. This happened after one particularly bad fight (in Tuscaloosa, of all places, which gave it, retroactively, the quality of a country song: the very name is plaintive and darkly comic, a geographic losing streak), during which we both genuinely thought we might break up. We did not, obviously, but we scared ourselves very badly. Afterward, we experienced a relief equal in size to that fear, but far more illuminating: we were, very definitely, *not* going to break up—not in Tuscaloosa, not right then, not anywhere, not ever.

That realization acted much as wedding vows are meant to do, shifting something fundamental between us. It became clear, almost immediately, that the fear of losing each other had fueled nearly all of our fights, turning ordinary misunderstandings and differences of opinion into unnecessary crises. Her insistence on self-soothing had had an element of the apocalyptic to it; in withdrawing from me, she was not only trying to let go of whatever was bothering her but also rehearsing life without me, trying to prove to herself that she would be fine if I left. Meanwhile, I rushed to resolve things because I had no illusion at all that I would be fine if she left, and no ability to calm down and recognize that she was not on the verge of doing so. But after Tuscaloosa, we realized—not abstractly, not intermittently, not only when all was well between us, but all the time and absolutely—that no one was leaving. She stopped bracing for it; I stopped reacting as if it were already happening. And just like that, the panic went out of our disputes, and something very much like levity entered them.

In this sense, love is the kind of problem that Carl Gauss, the mathematician, would have recognized: you may know with absolute certainty that you have the correct answer yet still need a long time to work out the details. Once you do, though, the solution will seem, as solutions so often do, obvious and elegant, and it will render the confusion that came before it borderline unimaginable. C. and I still disagree from time to time, and I hope we always will; the sovereignty of her mind, the way it challenges mine, is one of the things I cherish most about her, and I can't bear the thought of how impoverished my life would be without it. ("Nobody contradicts me now," Queen Victoria wrote after the death of her beloved husband, Prince Albert, "and the salt has gone out of my life.") Occasionally, those disagreements flare up into arguments, but these days we stick to the actual issue at hand, and generally work our way through it, if not always comically and tenderly, then at least sanely and quickly. As often as not, now, she steps toward me, to soothe or reconcile, and just as often, I step back—not to pull away from her, but because that is a good position from which to really see someone. *This is you,* I think, *being you,* and love her for it.

THE WINTER AFTER I first took C. back to Ohio with me, we returned to help my parents move out of the house where I grew up. This had been a long time coming. After my father's health had started to decline, my mother had begun lobbying for a smaller home, the kind with no stairs to fall down and less space to manage on their own. My father, while in theory not opposed to this plan, in practice had vetoed every place they visited. He liked their current house and declared himself comfortable in it; he did not declare, but all of us inferred, that he did not want to make so overt a concession to aging. It took five years for my mother to win him over.

By the standards of his generation—which, admittedly, were low ones—my father had always been relatively involved in household matters. In addition to classically masculine tasks like taking out the trash and mowing the lawn, he made lunch for my sister and me when we were too little to do so ourselves, helped put us to bed at night, did at least some of the cooking and dishes, loved to grocery shop, and, in his fifties, took over dinner duty entirely. Yet it was still my mother who, in ways aligned with their temperaments as well as their times, handled the lion's share of domestic work throughout their marriage. She made all the meals that my father did not, ironed, swept, scrubbed, and vacuumed, tracked what food and other items needed to be replaced, kept us in clothes and school supplies, did the laundry, hired babysitters, sorted out after-school activities and car pools and pick-up arrangements, took us to doctor and dentist appointments, took time off from work when we were sick, and generally handled the everyday stuff of keeping a house and making a home.

On top of all this, it had always fallen to my mother to find those homes in the first place. It was she who had done the work of both choosing and settling into each one: the apartment in Michigan where my parents lived when they were first married, the one in Cleveland where my sister was born, the modest house they moved into to make space for a second child, the grand one they bought once my father's career began to flourish. And so it was my mother who, beginning in her seventieth year, visited every viable piece of real estate on the market until my father, bowing to reality or simply to his extremely patient wife, finally conceded that the latest condo she had shown him seemed like a pretty decent place to live.

Then came the moving. Since my father was long past the stage where he could do any of the physical labor and my mother could no longer handle it all on her own, my sister and C. and I converged on Cleveland to help out. By then, C. and I knew each other well enough and had been back to Ohio often enough that I was no longer worried about the framed school pictures on the wall (which, anyway, she had taken one look at and loyally declared adorable) or anything else that the contents of the house might reveal about my past. And it was a good thing. Other than the internet, is there any richer source of potential embarrassment than a pack-rat parent and a childhood home? One afternoon, tasked with emptying the attic, we began going through an old steamer trunk that turned out to contain virtually every piece of my paper my sister or I had ever written on in childhood. C. fished them out one by one and, ignoring our laughter (plus the battered old stuffed animal I eventually threw at her), offered dramatic readings of dreadful grade school poetry and notes we'd passed in junior high and earnest fifth-grade book reports.

The next day, we laughed even harder when my sister, in the course of cleaning out the kitchen, found on top of the refrigerator an ancient kitchen witch—a cheery if somewhat deformed old lady perched atop a broom, meant to bring good luck to the home she adorned. By the looks of it, she had been acquired sometime around 1978 and forgotten sometime around 1984, which, give or take a few years, was turning out to be true of a considerable number of my parents' possessions. By then, my sister and C. and I were three days into what was starting to seem like a three-thousand-day task, and we were growing collectively more amused, aghast, and overwhelmed with the discovery of each successive object. The witch on her scraggly broom was, so to speak, the last straw. My mother was in the next room and none of us wanted to make her feel bad, so my sister waved it around wildly but mutely, with a look, somewhere between distress and triumph, that plainly said that she had found the definitive example of the problem we were facing: how to clean out a four-story home that had been continuously occupied without any serious de-junking for thirty-plus years. The effort to not draw my mother's attention somehow only added to the comedy of the moment; I had been sitting on the kitchen counter, like a teenager, and, doubled over, promptly slid off it.

It was good to laugh so much, and unexpected. Helping your aging parents move out of their longtime home is an exercise in watching the literal merge at every moment with the symbolic: the necessity of parting with so much all at once, the doors that close permanently behind them, the diminishing of the space they occupy in the world. I had thought, beforehand, that I would feel, in the midst of all this, a terrible two-way sadness, a sense of loss about the future as well as the past. But what I actually felt, along with the pleasure of being with my family, was tremendously lucky. I had learned, during my father's long decline, to be just as grateful for what didn't happen as for what did, and so I was relieved to be moving my parents out of that house while they were still there to laugh alongside us, before every hour we spent in it and every object we took out of it would have been steeped in grief.

It took several months, many more trips to Ohio, and countless excursions to Goodwill before that house was thoroughly empty and my parents were settled into their new home. In the end, despite all his resistance, it was an easy transition for my father. As usual, this was thanks to my mother, who managed to make the new place look remarkably like a miniature version of the old one. After dinner on their first night there, he settled into his preferred chair in the living room, the book he was reading on his lap and a glass of scotch on a familiar table next to him, and I sat across from him, marveling at how much he already seemed at home.

Meanwhile, during all of this packing and moving, C. and I were juggling an increasing number of homes of our own. When we met, I was renting that little carriage house in the Hudson Valley and she was renting a place on the Eastern Shore. A few months later, she bought a house down there, after a comic conversation in which she assured me that she was neither unsubtly signaling a lack of interest in dating me nor indicating that she would never move away from Maryland. The house had belonged to family friends who, like my parents, had grown too old to take care of it; the opportunity was too good and the mortgage too affordable to turn it down. Around that same time, she began working on a book set largely in the Deep South, which meant that I was either going to be spending a lot of time in small-town Alabama or a lot of time alone. I opted for the former, and we rented a furnished double-wide on a lake an hour or so from the Georgia line. We named the taxidermy deer in the dining room Nickajack (for a breakaway region of the South that declined to side with the Confederacy during the Civil War) and read *Midnight in the Garden of Good and Evil* aloud to each other while making dinner and sat on the porch in the morning drinking coffee and watching the fog lift off the lake. While she went out to do her reporting, I stayed home and wrote and went for long runs in the steep piney hills surrounding the water; on days off, we got in the car and went in search of adventure.

The car was, in effect, another home in those days. We would drive from Alabama to Maryland (C., as I said, loves to drive), from Maryland to New York, from New York back down south again in an epic stretch of country music and coffee and twenty-four-hour biscuit joints. When we were not traveling toward one home or another we were traveling for work, hers or mine, or heading to this or that place we had always wanted to see, or making time to visit various far-flung friends. We tried to keep the car reasonably clean on those journeys, but its contents soon came to reflect the extent to which we really did live in it: hair ties, paper towels, a toothbrush and toothpaste, trail mix, sunscreen, allergy meds, a salt shaker (that was for C.), a blanket and pillow (I sometimes napped), water bottles, thermoses, a converter to charge our laptops (I once wrote an entire article between the Eastern Shore and Gaffney, South Carolina), books, magazines, swimsuits, rain jackets, a first aid kit, an annual pass to the national parks, and three full file boxes of C.'s reporting, which permanently occupied the same place in the trunk and served as a kind of security blanket, in case for some reason we were detained on a back road for two years and she needed to meet her book deadline.

From time to time, this lifestyle proved maddening. Inevitably, there were days when we realized that we had left my running shoes behind when we'd struck off for Alabama, or that the book we were looking for in New York was down in Maryland, or that an event we wanted to attend in one location was the day after we planned to leave for another. For the most part, though, it was incredibly fun—and something more than fun, too. C. and I were, I knew, extremely fortunate. Because we can both do our jobs from anywhere, we were never really in a long-distance relationship; we were in a relationship in which, together, we traveled long distances. And all those highways, all those miles, the hours of talking in the car, the country in its endless interestingness unfurling there beside us—all of this took us someplace else, too, farther and farther down all kinds of roads and ever closer to each other. And then, fifteen months into this lovely nomadic life, in what started out seeming like just another road trip, we drove back to Ohio because my father had been admitted to the hospital for atrial fibrillation.

In the nights before he died, C. and I slept on a fold-out sofa in the sitting room of the condo, a makeshift curtain drawn across its doorway. Or, anyway, we tried to sleep; for the most part I lay there awake, exhausted yet insomniac, unable to look either fully at or fully away from the coming loss. Each morning when I woke up, I had to orient myself all over again in the new home. My mother and father had lived there scarcely six months; now, with each passing day, it seemed less and less likely that he would ever return. When the time came to decide what to do, my mother, sad and calm and clear, told us that she wanted what she also did not want at all: to let my father go. I marveled at her strength then, and all throughout the time that he was dying, but grief will find a foothold anyway, and anywhere. The day after we moved him to hospice care, I came upon my mother in her bedroom, terribly undone. When I asked if something specific was upsetting her, she gestured toward the bathroom and told me, through her tears, that my father had barely gotten to use the handicap-accessible shower she'd had installed there for him.

Less than a week later, he was gone. After the arrangements were handled, after the memorial service was over, after C. had packed our bag and carried it out to the hall, I put my arms around my mother and could barely bring myself to let her go. I stood there in the doorway holding on to her, feeling stunned and drained and staring blankly over her shoulder into the living room. I remembered, then, what I'd thought the first time I'd seen the condo after she and my father had moved in: that it looked almost exactly like home, except that so much of it was no longer there.

It is, I must say, almost beyond belief what sometimes lurks around life's next bend. C. bundled me into the car, nearly as unresponsive as if I were one of the boxes in the trunk, and drove me back to Maryland. It was past midnight when we got in. The mail was piled chest-high on a table in the living room. The cats twined ecstatically around our legs. I stumbled upstairs, overwhelmed by a colossal, grief-drenched fatigue, and began to get ready for bed. It was then that I glanced down and noticed tiny dots on my bare feet. I bent to look closer and thought a series of dim, desperate, incredulous things. Our cats do not go outside and we had never had a problem with them before. Yet by the time C. heard me call her and came upstairs, I could see that everything around me—the floors, the pillows, the blanket, my feet: all of it was covered in fleas.

We looked at each other for a very long moment. And while this is neither a practical nor a palatable suggestion, I do think, in retrospect, that if you ever want to know if you are in the right relationship, you might try the combination of an eight-hour drive, twelve forty-five in the morning, fresh grief, and fleas. C. took both my hands in hers, looked me in my shell-shocked eyes, and offered to get us a hotel room. I shook my head; the one thing I wanted, more than anything, more even than sleep, was to feel like I had a home. And so, as calmly as if it were high noon and she had just developed an interest in practical entomology, she began googling what to do about an infestation of fleas. Meanwhile I stood there uselessly, my sorrow suspended like something hideous in a murky solution of disbelief. The only other feeling I could access was an abiding gratitude that I had not walked into that house and that situation— that whole appalling, absurd, overwhelming situation—all alone.

Shortly thereafter, and for the first time in my life, I found myself almost equally grateful for the fact that there is such a thing in this world as a twenty-four-hour big-box store. It was inside one of these, halfway down the pet aisle, that my exhausted inward needle swung abruptly from meltdown to mirth. The next thing I felt was a longing that I knew would be with me for the rest of my days: I wanted to tell my father what had happened. My mother would feel awful for us, I knew, but my father— Standing there next to C., holding a bottle of flea shampoo, I started to laugh. My father, feigning perfect seriousness, would have said, "I've always told you you should get rid of those terrible cats." He would have reminded me about the world's shortest poem about fleas ("Adam / had 'em") and understood its relevance: how even at the extremes of human experience, rejoicing or grieving, in paradise or newly expelled from it, we are still just another lowly creature at the mercy of the world. The thought buoyed me up somehow, and in the car on the way home I felt, despite everything, more human than I had in weeks. In another two hours, the floors were treated, the terrible cats were angry and clean, the old linens were in the laundry, fresh sheets were on the bed, and we were in it.

That was the night I decided I no longer wanted more than one home. It took effort, in my disordered, exhausted, past-caring condition, not to immediately say as much to C. They tell you, however, not to make major life changes while you are grieving (never mind that grief is often occasioned by exactly the kinds of circumstances that require them), and so, although I knew what I wanted, I waited. But once the worst sorrow had ebbed and the darkness of fall and winter had lifted, we returned to the Hudson Valley to once again begin the project of packing up a home. By then, two years had passed since I had walked C. back from lunch with me and we had stood there together outside the house, admiring the seedlings just starting to come up in the garden, not quite knowing yet what we were doing.

That house was fun to pack up, too, though easier and more exciting. By the night before the move, all but the barest necessities were ready to go—disassembled, swaddled in blankets, stacked in boxes by the door. We got take-out Indian food, watched *Raiders of the Lost Ark* on C.'s laptop, stayed up late attending to the last loose ends, then fell asleep on a mattress on the floor, the bed frame already taken apart and propped against the wall downstairs. By noon the next day, the moving truck was loaded. We pulled its rear door closed and walked to town and had lunch at the café where we first met, pausing at the end to get a couple of coffees for the road. Then we walked back home and down the little hill to the carriage house and stuck our heads in its front door. I had lived in that place for a dozen years by then, and had loved everything about it. But looking around its emptiness, I felt no pang of nostalgia or loss. "A cicada shell," the poet Bashō once wrote in a beautiful little haiku. "It sang itself / utterly away."

IN CLASSICAL MYTHOLOGY, Eros had a younger brother, Anteros—the god not of love alone but of love requited. The story goes that the infant Eros was sickly and weak, and so, on the advice of one of the Titans, Aphrodite bore another child to keep him company. After that, whenever Eros was alone, he grew listless and ill, but whenever the two boys were together, they thrived. Once they reached adulthood, Eros became eternally associated with the more harrowing aspects of falling in love: with longing, with absence, with thwarted passion. His chosen means of inflicting desire—arrows, fires, fevers, hammers, hurricanes—were coercive and painful, and everywhere he went, he sowed mischief and chaos. (According to some accounts, he caused the married Helen to fall in love with Paris, thereby helping to trigger the Trojan War.) By contrast, Anteros was loyal and tender, except when avenging mistreated lovers. Conceived to keep his brother from being lonely, he went on to protect others from the same fate.

An enigmatic figure even in his own time, Anteros has

vanished almost entirely from our collective memory of the ancient pantheon. That is a telling elision; we no longer animate, literally or figuratively, the experience of requited love. Yet it is there that all of our romantic happiness lies—because, as the reputation of Eros makes clear, love experienced alone is not a pleasant thing. If its many chroniclers from the time of the Greeks to the present are to be believed, the longing for someone else, when unfulfilled, is primarily a destructive force, dangerous for the lover and potentially just as bad for the rest of the world.

Requited love is the opposite of that. Overall, if not at every moment, it is sustaining, generous, exhilarating, and fulfilling. But, like Anteros, it is largely overlooked in our culture, victim of the general consensus that happiness is pleasant but uninteresting. "Happy families are all alike," Tolstoy declared, famously and dismissively, at the beginning of *Anna Karenina;* "every unhappy family is unhappy in its own way." It is a wonderful novel, but a very strange claim. For one thing, Tolstoy's contention is at odds with experience. By age nine, I knew how dramatically my own happy family differed from that of one of my best friends, whose parents were devout, outdoorsy, slightly crunchy, and so constitutionally tranquil that their prevailing conversational tone was the murmur—a familial ecosystem as different from my own nerdy, rowdy, ebullient one as a tidepool is from a tropical rain forest. For another, it is at odds with logic. In what possible ways, for what possible reasons, would unhappiness be more rich and varied than its antithesis? As often as not, anguish is produced by the eradication of joy, so that the one can hardly be more specific and interesting than the other; and as for mere everyday misery, that generally takes the form of a long and tedious bleakness.

What Simone Weil wrote of evil is also true of suffering: the imaginary kind may be "romantic and varied," but the real kind is "gloomy, monotonous, barren, boring."

Despite all this, happiness routinely gets not only less attention but also more criticism than its opposite number. Contemporary thinkers sometimes dismiss it as a shallow fixation of modern life, but to condemn it on those grounds is to mistake it for proximate but different phenomena—either superficial forms of itself, like amusement and pleasure, or superficial means of trying to achieve it, from substance abuse to so-called retail therapy. Aristotle, by contrast, regarded happiness as the "supreme good," and understood it as something less like transient gratification than like full human flourishing, inextricable from thoughtfulness, inextricable from virtue.

You might imagine that, however much happiness is sidelined elsewhere, it would at least play a central role in love stories, but that is seldom the case. Instead, the vision of love in literature is often bleak, emphasizing (as Tolstoy did) suffering over gladness, turbulence over contentment, and tragedy over romance. There are plenty of exceptions to this rule—from Austen and Balzac to fairy tales, rom-coms, and romance novels—but even where the vision of love is rosier, the focus is generally on obtaining it, not sustaining it: "happily ever after" is the ending, not the story. The implication is that happiness is a static state, with nothing much to be said about it, and that love, once you've found it, becomes boring—or, worse, becomes something that isn't really love at all. This is an ancient and persistent notion: that romantic love is really just desire, and desire is always a longing for something you don't already have. That's why most love stories tell us so much about searching for love yet so little about what it is like to finally find it. Boy meets girl, boy loses girl, boy gets girl: even in the upbeat version, the tale ends with the getting, precisely at the moment when most of us believe love really begins.

Writers of romantic stories, in other words, generally dwell on love's beginning or on its end but largely neglect its middle—which, per our general lack of interest in happiness, they seek to make as short as possible. But actual lovers do the exact opposite: they seek to make the middle as long as they can; they wish it would go on forever. As that suggests, and as anyone who has ever been in love knows, it is, in fact, perfectly possible to desire what we already have. I have longed for C. when she is right there in the same room with me but annoyed or distracted; I have longed for her when she is out of town and I'm having a lousy day; I have longed for her when she is asleep in my arms and I am in the grip of existential dread, desperate to keep having her, unable to stop worrying about losing her. Requited lovers don't suffer from a lack of desire, only from a fundamental change in its form. We do not desire the new, that default yearning of contemporary culture. We desire only more of the same. Here is Robert Frost, capturing the feeling perfectly, in a little poem called "Devotion":

> The heart can think of no devotion
> Greater than being shore to the ocean—
> Holding the curve of one position,
> Counting an endless repetition.

I have thought of those lines more often than I can say, at night when C. and I are curled up in bed together, her body wrapped around mine, her long fingers holding mine against my heart, or on mornings when I wake up to her magic eyes and bright morning cheer and smile through my sleepiness. *All I ever want is this,* I think in those moments and countless others, *over and over and over again for a hundred thousand years.* That is the essence of requited love and, surely, the luckiest of all conditions: to wish only for what we already have.

But i have not yet said anything about the first time C. took me back to her childhood home. This was during the autumn after we met, some months after we got that flat tire on the way to Ohio. We left the Hudson Valley late one afternoon and drove south, on roads that grew progressively smaller the closer we got to our destination. By the time we crossed the county line, night had fallen. The crickets were so loud we could hear them from inside the car. I leaned forward in my seat to look up at the sky, as dense with stars as if a box full of the universe had tipped and spilled out overhead. Below them, the occasional stand of trees formed a patch of darker darkness, marking the meandering path of a creek or a windbreak at the edge of a field. Other than that, the land stretched out unbroken all around us, an enormous coastal plain that, sixty miles farther east, surrendered to the sea.

Later, after I moved in with C., I would come to know those roads by day, the crops speeding past on both sides, their even furrows making a kind of stop-motion photography. And I would watch them fly past, too, with the seasons, wheat giving way to soybeans, soybeans to sorghum, sorghum to field corn that, by August, stands so tall you can't see around the corner at intersections. Now and again silos rise up in the distance. At the junctions where dirt roads meet paved ones, honor-system farm stands advertise fresh tomatoes and homemade jam and hot peppers and peaches. On dark winter mornings, the shorn fields crunch underfoot with frost and fog hovers just above the ground, like a blanket if something had spirited away the bed beneath it.

Tidewater Maryland, they call it, and it's true: all that farmland is always just inches away from becoming marshland. In heavy rains, the crops rise up from low temporary lakes and serene little wood ducks paddle across the fields atop their own reflections. To the east, the gray Atlantic heaves and booms. To the west, the half-salt, half-sweet waters of the bay lap steadily away at the delicate lacework of the coastline. In between, a dozen and more rivers divvy up the land—the Pocomoke, the Nanticoke, the Miles, the Wye, the Wicomico, the Sassafras, the Choptank, the Little Choptank, the Tred Avon, too many others to name. The tributaries that flow out of them are said to number close to ten thousand.

Loss diminishes the world; finding makes it richer, more abundant, more interesting. Since C. and I met, I have fallen in love, also, with the wind-tossed, high-gloss green of winter wheat—to my mind, the most beautiful shade of green on a planet full of beautiful shades of green. I have stood by the side of a field and watched hundreds of snow geese take flight, as if departing our mortal world for their own enchanted kingdom. I have moved to a part of the country I'd never heard of before and, leaning into the wind on afternoon runs where the air rolls across the unobstructed land with the force of the sea, felt an exhilaration as pure as any I've felt on top of a mountain. I have grown close to C.'s parents and sisters and extended family, gone to church with them on Easter morning and tucked presents under their tree for Christmas Day. I have found a home as wonderful as the one into which I was born, and as impossible to imagine beforehand.

In one of my favorite passages ever written about love, James Baldwin asks his readers to imagine that they are from Chicago, know nothing about the island of Hong Kong, and have no desire at all to visit it. Now, he writes, "pretend that some convulsion, sometimes called accident, throws you into connection with a man or a woman who lives in Hong Kong; and that you fall in love. Hong Kong will immediately cease to be a name and become the center of your life." He goes on:

> If your lover lives in Hong Kong and cannot get to Chicago, it will be necessary for you to go to Hong Kong. Perhaps you will spend your life there, and never see Chicago again. And you will, I assure you, as long as space and time divide you from anyone you love, discover a great deal about shipping routes, airlanes, earthquake, famine, disease, and war. And you will always know what time it is in Hong Kong, for you love someone who lives there. And love will simply have no choice but to go into battle with space and time and, furthermore, to win.

I would go even further and say that the moment you meet your beloved, the battle with space and time has already been won. C. is not from Hong Kong, and I am not from Chicago. Still, we were born far enough apart in time and lived far enough apart in space to make it feel improbable that the two of us, each wholly free to fall in love with the other, each mysteriously and powerfully inclined to do so, should have met on Main Street that lovely spring day— "neither an inch nor half a globe too far," as the poet Wisława Szymborska once wrote, "neither a minute nor aeons too early."

To what convulsion, to what accident, do we owe that encounter? For those, like C., who believe in God, or in a universe otherwise ordered in part by watchful and benevolent forces, such meetings, like all wonderful finds, have a straightforward explanation: they are blessings, godsends, miracles. The lover and the beloved were meant for each other—indeed, in a very literal sense, made for each other— and their encounter was never *not* going to happen. In that vein, you sometimes hear couples say that they were destined to meet. But among those of us without that faith, and perhaps even among some of the devout as well, I suspect that the opposite feeling is at least as common: a kind of amazed gratitude, given the wild contingency of life, that such an unlikely thing could ever come to pass. That is how I feel: that finding one's beloved is an "Astonishment," to borrow the title of that Szymborska poem, because, cosmically speaking, there is so much time and space in which not to do so.

Never have I felt this more strongly than on that first visit with C. to the Eastern Shore. The closer we got to her hometown, the more unlikely it started to seem that we had ever met. Other than a trip to Baltimore in my teens, I had never been to Maryland before, knew almost nothing about it, and had only belatedly learned that part of it was out on a peninsula, removed from the rest; when C. first told me where she lived, I had struggled to place the region on a map. Now, driving through it, I did not find it any easier to process our location. It seemed impossible that Washington, D.C., was only ninety minutes away; the place we were in felt as remote from the nation's capital as Nebraska.

These days, the Eastern Shore is my home as well, and in the years that I have lived here, I have spent so much time in the house where C. grew up that it has become a kind of home to me, too. Her mother taught me to pick crabs on its front porch; her father taught me to use a miter saw out in its shed. I have helped repaint the bedrooms and reorganize the crawl space and clean up downed limbs outside after a storm. I have sat in the kitchen shelling peas, sprawled on the couch watching television, brought potato salad and corn on the cob when family friends were coming over for a cookout. Some days I drop by just to pick up a spare key or leave a plate of biscuits; other times, I laze around for most of a weekend. I have been there in dress clothes and pajamas, have gone there to share good news and to find solace in grief.

But on that first visit, I came as a stranger, new to the Shore, new to her family, still very much in that phase of love I described as a yearning for information. For many months by then, I had wanted to see the home where C. grew up; now she led me up the walkway and through the door. The archaeological dig out back had long since been filled in and plowed over, but all the artifacts she'd found while excavating it were still inside, neatly organized in a display case she fished out from under the bed. The bookshelves her father had built for her remained in her childhood room, although there was not much else to see there, since her younger sister had redecorated after C. left. In the living room, I stood for a while in front of a shelf full of photographs of her as a kid, adorable and serious-eyed and scrawny as an urchin: sitting on the church steps with her sisters in identical Easter dresses; standing on a dock holding up a freshly caught rockfish almost as tall as she was; muddy-kneed in a Little League uniform.

I could have looked at them forever, looked at a thousand more. My farmer's daughter, my Rhodes scholar, my devout Christian, with the fierce intellect and the faithful heart, who can recite Eliot and read Greek and run a wood splitter and set a trotline: before we met, if someone had given me pen and paper and ten thousand years and asked me to describe the person I would one day fall in love with, I would never, in all that time, have dreamed up anyone like her. "Where did you come from?" I sometimes asked C. in those days, in awe and gratitude. Standing there in her house, in the very center of a certain kind of answer to that question, the deeper one did not seem any less mysterious. How, from here, had she come to be who she was? How, from here, had she come to be with me?

What an astonishing thing it is to find someone. Loss may alter our sense of scale, reminding us that the world is overwhelmingly large while we are incredibly tiny. But finding does the same; the only difference is that it makes us marvel rather than despair. In all the vast reaches of space, among all of life's infinite permutations, out of all the trajectories and possibilities and people on the planet, here I was, in this house, following along beside C. as she took my hand and led me out of the living room and into the kitchen, where, she told me, there was something else she wanted me to see. I picked it up off the hearth by the woodstove and examined it, not sure what I was looking at. It was a meteorite, she explained, that her father had found after watching it fall in the fields outside when he was a boy.

III.
And

Long before C.'s father was born—long before any of us were born—another meteorite struck the earth not far from his future home. This was toward the end of the Eocene epoch, some thirty-five million years ago, a time when much of the Mid-Atlantic region really was mid-Atlantic. Because the eastern coastline of North America fell well inland of its current location, parts of what are now New Jersey and Virginia, together with all of Delaware and the Eastern Shore of Maryland, lay beneath a shallow ocean.

For the previous twenty million years, the earth had been extremely hot. Under an atmosphere thick with carbon dioxide and methane, seawater exceeded one hundred degrees, alligators crawled around Canada, and palm trees cast their shadows on the fertile soil of the Arctic. By the late Eocene, global temperatures had begun to moderate, but in North America, lush tropical rain forests still stretched from Appalachia to the Atlantic Ocean. Like rain forests today, these teemed with life: frogs and toads and salamanders, butterflies and dragonflies and golden beetles, dwarf ungulates and dawn horses and miniature tapirs and scores of other prehistoric creatures.

Who knows what they registered, if anything, when the object that would put an end to most of them passed overhead. At all events, they had only a few seconds to do so. The meteorite was roughly two miles wide and a billion tons; it came in from the north, at fifty thousand miles per hour, covered the distance from the Arctic Circle to Virginia in three minutes, and smashed into the Atlantic Ocean just west of what is now Cape Charles. The ocean barely slowed it down; it vaporized millions of tons of water, displaced millions of tons more, and roared on through layers of sediment and stone until finally, five miles beneath the bottom of the sea, it slammed into the basement rock of the earth. On impact, it obliterated itself, opening up a crater a mile deep and twice the size of Rhode Island and igniting a massive explosion. Ash and burning rocks rose some three hundred thousand feet into the air, strewing bits of meteorite-made glass across more than four million square miles of North America and the Atlantic Ocean. Meanwhile, the swath of that ocean that had been displaced rose up in an enormous fortress of waves, well over a thousand feet high, collapsed under its own weight, and began speeding off toward the coast. The resulting tsunami poured inland across a hundred miles of Virginia before finally dissipating its remaining energy high up on the granite sides of the Blue Ridge Mountains.

Time passed. Day turned to dusk, dusk to night, night to dawn. The fires extinguished themselves. Ferns and saplings took root in the rotting bodies of downed trees. The earth carried on in its usual course around the sun. A year passed. A century passed. Lava boiled up from the seafloor, creating new continent stuff, nudging the land above it into sluggish motion. Volcanoes erupted, clogging river valleys and lake beds with layers of ash. Millennia passed. The rain forests receded, replaced by stands of white oak and beech and pine. Saber-toothed tigers and dire wolves roamed among them, hunting giant sloths and juvenile mammoths. Another year went by, a million times. The eastern coastline of North America rose up out of the sea and dried out. Megalodons trawled the waters beyond it, the ocean sliding over their backs the way a river turns flat and calm over a large, smooth stone. Inland, the forests filled up with white-tailed deer, the first or second or third of the next four hundred thousand generations. Half a globe away, in the Rift Valley of Africa, a kind of primate wholly new to the planet took, for the first time, to its feet.

More time passed. The earth, already colder than it once was, started to cool some more. The polar sea solidified. Ice began to spread across the planet. There were glaciers in New Zealand and Tasmania, glaciers on the islands of Sardinia and Majorca, glaciers in Columbus, Ohio, and Philadelphia, Pennsylvania. Across North America, the Laurentide Ice Sheet covered five million square miles, in some places to a depth of ten thousand feet. The ice made land where there used to be water, and countless creatures in search of new homes, including humans, walked across it.

And then, sometime around twenty thousand years ago, the temperature started to climb again, and all that ice began to melt. With water pouring off the glaciers and ice caps and out of every swollen delta, the sea began to rise. It mounted steadily over low-lying coastal areas and flowed up through the mouths of rivers, drowning them beneath the ocean. In the Mid-Atlantic, four of those rivers—today called the York, the James, the Susquehanna, and the Rappahannock—had long converged on the same spot. Drawn downward by gravity, they emptied out into the remains of an ancient crater, one cut so deep into the planet's crust that not even thirty-five million years of slurry and sediment compacting on top of it could bring it level with the surrounding land. When the ice melted and the sea rose up, it followed the course carved by those rivers, flooding the land above what is known, today, as the Chesapeake Bay impact crater.

The meteorite helped dictate its location, and the rising ocean filled it with water, but it was the existence of a peninsula just to the east that made the Chesapeake a bay. When it first began taking shape, nearly two million years ago, that peninsula was just a narrow barrier spit, its eastern face turned to the full force of the sea. Over the ensuing millennia, ocean levels fluctuated, alternately depositing silt on the spit to elongate it when the waters ran high and, when they dropped, exposing a broader swath of the land, a swampy composite of sand and gravel and peat and clay. Wind and wave kept on shaping it, adding and eroding, washing up and scouring away. Off its coast, small islands emerged and vanished, then reemerged, like diving birds, in new places.

Only about three thousand years ago did the peninsula assume its current shape, curling like a comma off the coast of mainland America. Although it is just a hundred and seventy miles long from top to tail, it has over twelve thousand miles of shoreline, more than the entire West Coast of the United States. All along its own western edge, the land goes fractal, the main peninsula spawning smaller ones, their elaborately scalloped edges eddying into the bay. Just beyond those, where the contest between land and water reaches a temporary draw, islands dot the bay—Poplar Island and Carpenter Island, Smith and St. George and Solomons and dozens more. Out on the very tip of one of those, just beyond a little fishing village, the land narrows to a point, water surrounding it on three sides. Egrets and herons stalk the shallows all around it, slender as the reeds that hide them. Below them, broken bits of shell shift with the sand, and smooth round rocks shine upward through the water like wishes in a well. On sunny days, diamonds of light from the waves slosh in and out of the shade from the willows and walnut trees lining the shore, forming a wide dappled edge where one element meets another and where, one beautiful May afternoon, C. and I got married.

Languages, like landmasses, change shape over time. Until the late nineteenth century, the final character of the English alphabet was not the letter Z but a word: "and." That word was written—on countless slates and blackboards and grade school primers—as "&," so that the whole sequence looked like this:

A B C D E F G H I J K L M N O P Q R S T U V W X Y Z &

The twenty-seventh of those symbols dates back to ancient Rome, when scribes, resorting to cursive to write more rapidly, linked the two letters in "εt," the Latin word for "and." You can still make out those letters today in certain fancier versions of the character, like this one:

&

As Latin took hold throughout Christendom, becoming the dominant and in some cases the only written language, the "&" spread along with it. When Latin eventually receded (thanks in part to Dante with his vernacular poetry, Gutenberg with his vernacular printing, and Martin Luther with his vernacular preaching), its script was left behind, complete with the "&"—a kind of philological fossil, still written as the Roman scribes had done but pronounced in whatever way the locals said "and."

It makes sense that this stray character got appended to the English alphabet. Students had to learn to read and write it, after all, and it was at least as tricky to form as *R* or *Z*. The fact that it represents an entire word was hardly disqualifying; so can *A* and *I* and even *O* (as in "O Come, All Ye Faithful" and "O death, where is thy sting?"). But the "&" did present a unique problem. If you recite the alphabet with it stuck to the end, as schoolchildren across the English-speaking world were routinely required to do, you sound as if you are leaving your listener hanging: ". . . X, Y, Z, and." And what? It's not true, no matter what old-fashioned grammarians might tell you, that you shouldn't start a sentence with "and," but ending something that way is a different story. To solve this problem, students were taught to use the Latin phrase *per se,* meaning "in itself," to indicate that they meant the character, not the word. Thus instead of saying "X, Y, Z, and," they dutifully said, "X, Y, Z, and *per se* and"—a phrase that, over time, grew blurry from repetition. It is our language, then, that turned the Latin "&" into the ampersand.

It is not clear exactly when "and" migrated out of the alphabet, although it was probably hastened along by a music publisher in Boston named Charles Bradlee, who, in 1835, appropriated a Mozart piano variation, availed himself of the English alphabet for lyrics, and proceeded to make an enduring hit with the under-seven set. Bradlee's version ended at Z, which was either a cause or an effect (or both) of the gradual disappearance of "&" from the English alphabet. Today, typesetters and font designers regard the ampersand not as a letter but as punctuation, and the rest of us regard "and" as only a word. Yet there is something apt about its former status as part of the alphabet— a covert acknowledgment of how early we learn it and how much we need it, how elemental it is to the ways we think and speak.

That importance begins with the role that "and" plays as a kind of linguistic superglue, capable of binding together almost anything. You probably remember from grade school that it is a conjunction—a coming together, a way of joining two or more things. Dozens of other words also serve that purpose, including *but, yet, for, nor, before, after, because, although, if, so, once, since, until, unless, while, whereas,* and *whenever.* Almost all of these other conjunctions reveal something about the relationship between the things that are being joined. Some of them link a cause to its effect: "We talked all afternoon, *so* I was late getting home." Others set up a contrast or exception: "We talked all afternoon, *yet* still had more to say"; "We talked all night *but* did not touch." Others present a rationale: "I couldn't bear to leave, *for* I found her fascinating." Others indicate an arrangement in space or time: "She called me *after* she got home"; "I accompanied her *wherever* she went." Others offer an alternative: "We could go for a walk *or* go to a movie." And still others introduce a contingency: "I will come for dinner *if* you are free"; "I will stay *unless* you want me to go."

"And" does none of these things. It is a connection made of nothing but connection; two things, three things, ten things coexist in a sentence, but grammar is mute on the subject of what, other than that single word, might bind them. This no-strings-attached combinatory power makes it a particularly easy conjunction to master: of all the ways we can put the world together, "and" is the most fundamental, the first and simplest knot we learn to tie. Young children, who may not grasp the specific relationships implied by other conjunctions, are fluent and profligate users of this one. From the plot of *Frozen* to the first day of kindergarten, life as little kids narrate it is just one long string of "and then—and then—and then."

This apparent simplicity makes "and" an easy word to overlook, a fact that William James pauses to note in a strange and wonderful passage in *The Principles of Psychology*. In the middle of writing about the stream of consciousness, which was his term for the constant flow of thoughts in the mind, he suddenly mixes his metaphors, shifting from an image of thought as a river to an image of thought as a bird. Like birds, he observes, our thoughts are sometimes in flight and sometimes perching, but we only ever observe them when they've alighted somewhere. He calls these perches the "substantive" parts of thought: the nouns and verbs and adjectives, which we fix our minds on when we think about the things we're thinking. The other, "transitive" parts of thought flit past without our notice. Yet they are what gives language its sense, by establishing its relations, and they are as distinct from one another as "tornado" is from "celebrity" is from "roast beef." "We ought to say a feeling of *and,* a feeling of *if,* a feeling of *but,* and a feeling of *by,*" James wrote, "quite as readily as we say a feeling of *blue* or a feeling of *cold.*"

What, then, is the feeling of *and*? Above all, it is a feeling of association, a subtle awareness that two or more things have been brought into relationship. It doesn't matter whether those things are linked by affinity, animosity, or difference; Cain and Abel are bound together as tightly as Romeo and Juliet, and both are bound as tightly as apples and oranges. It doesn't even matter if they have no intrinsic link at all, because the effect of joining them with "and" is to create one. Chimpanzees and orangutans and baboons and spider monkeys have an inherent connection. Cabbages and kings did not, until Lewis Carroll put the "and" between them.

That semantic versatility reflects an existential truth. Our chronic condition involves experiencing many things all at once—some of them intrinsically related, some of them compatible, some of them contradictory, and some of them having nothing to do with one another at all, beyond being crowded together in our own awareness. Even if we try, we can hardly ever experience something all by itself, as James pointed out. His fellow psychologists treated "simple sensations"—one sight, one sound, one smell—as the atomic units of thought, which they advised studying in isolation to try to understand the mind as a whole. But "no one ever had a simple sensation by itself," James objected: we do not experience the feeling of heat separate from sunlight or a stovetop, from awareness of our own bodies, from the sound of waves or of our mother screaming. "Consciousness, from our natal day, is of a teeming multiplicity of objects and relations," he wrote, "and what we call simple sensations are results of discriminative attention, pushed often to a very high degree." His point was that his colleagues had it backward. Far from being the most basic activity of the mind, experiencing something in isolation is an effortful exception to the rule.

We all know this, because we have all tried to experience something in isolation, an exercise that promptly reveals the extent to which our minds are perpetual "and" machines. Even when you are attempting to focus on just one thing, such as the paragraph you are reading, or attempting to focus on nothing, as when meditating or trying to fall asleep, your brain is forever spitting out other things as well: items on your To Do list, anxiety about an upcoming doctor's appointment, the memory of something embarrassing you said the day before, the itchiness of the mosquito bite on your ankle, the lyrics to "Raised on Robbery."

And it is not just the background hubbub of the mind that throws the world into constant conjunction. Life, too, is a perpetual "and" machine, reliably delivering us a mixture of things to experience all at once. It is perfectly possible, in the course of any given hour, to be charmed by your nine-year-old and infuriated by your twelve-year-old and worried about an upcoming job interview and also worried about global climate change. This endless clamor sometimes produces difficult juxtapositions, because life, like "and," is indifferent to what it connects. Maybe your own personal circumstances are the best they've ever been but your nation is in crisis; maybe your brand-new baby daughter looks just like her grandmother but that grandmother is suffering from Alzheimer's and cannot recognize either one of you. Contrasts like these proliferate both around us and within us: you adore your brother but he drives you crazy; you despise your ex-husband but love beyond description the children you wouldn't have without him. We all have mixed experiences, mixed emotions, mixed motives, even mixed selves. The most cheerful among us is not consistently happy, and the best among us is not consistently good.

We are all, as my beloved Lutheran likes to say, *simul justus et peccator:* at once righteous and sinning.

In everyday life, we seldom fully focus on conjunctions like these, any more than we focus on the word "and." Yet multiple simultaneous experiences and emotions are so common that by the time we reach adulthood, the very fabric of our life is made of patchwork. We know by then that the world is full of beauty and grandeur and also wretchedness and suffering; we know that people are kind and funny and brilliant and brave and also petty and irritating and horrifically cruel. In short, we know that, as Philip Roth once put it, "Life *is* and." He meant that we do not live, for the most part, in a world of either/or. We live with both at once, with many things at once—everything connected to its opposite, everything connected to everything.

I ASKED C. TO marry me on Ash Wednesday. It was an accident—not the asking, the timing. The asking had been on my mind for the better part of two years. I had known I would someday do so since midway through our second date, and for a long time, both of us had talked about the future in terms that made it perfectly clear we planned to share it. As a practical matter, though, it had first come up when my father was in the hospital, dying. One day, after we had been sitting with him for hours, C. took me outside for a walk. It was a breezy, beautiful afternoon, and the vivid contrast of life outside the ICU—the seagull sound of young children at play, the spray from that fountain I liked gusting sidewise into rainbows, the windblown canopies of maple trees alternating green and silver against a brilliant blue sky:

all this made me register, for the first time, that my father was truly going to leave this world, that whatever happened in it from here on out would not be seen by him. I could not say out loud what I felt, but it must have been obvious, because C. put her arms around me and told me that if I wanted to, we could go procure the necessary paperwork and get married in his hospital room. I knew what she was offering, and I understood its generosity and gravity, but I shook my head into her shoulder. I did not want to marry in haste, for any reason; I did not want her family and all of our friends to miss the occasion so that my father could share it, if indeed he still could; and I did not want—although in this I really had no other choice—to mingle so much sorrow with so much joy.

So we did not wed that week, or say anything more about it for some time. But later that fall, I called my widowed mother and told her that I was planning to ask C. to marry me. She was thrilled, but she laughed out loud when I told her why else I was calling. I didn't think C. would want a conventional engagement ring, I explained, but I wanted to give her something meaningful from our family, and I wondered if my grandmother—my mother's mother, that fierce force of nature who had died at ninety-five—might have left behind any appropriate jewelry. My mother told me that I was welcome to all of it but that she couldn't imagine I would want any of it, and immediately I saw her point. My grandmother had been exceptionally glamorous in her day; she had Amelia Earhart bravura and Elizabeth Taylor looks, but although she was about as patrician as a middle-class Jew could be, her taste in jewelry ran to things that could be admired from down the block. My mother was right: there was no way C. would want to be seen in any of it. I was still registering that reality and thinking about other options when she said, quite serenely, Why don't you give her Daddy's wedding ring?

My father's wedding ring: the last time I had thought about it was in the hospital, when my mother, warned about possible swelling in his hands, had preemptively removed it and put it in her purse. It was identical to hers, and unusual. Although my parents were not remotely bohemian, they had gone in search of something unique when they'd decided to get married, and had settled on broad gold bands with a scalloped edge and a distinctive cable-like engraving. When I was young, I thought they looked like little crowns; as an adult, I found them somehow both ancient and art deco. Now I pictured C. wearing the one from my father—not as a ring but as a necklace, the V of it falling just below her collarbones—and could not imagine anything more perfect. I hadn't thought to wonder what my mother had done with it since his death, but it suddenly occurred to me that perhaps she had kept it in her purse all that time, or placed it by her bedside, or started wearing it herself, and I worried out loud that surely she must want to keep it. No, she replied, I want C. to have it, and I know that Dad would have wanted that, too. I called up my sister, concerned that she might want the ring for herself, or simply not want it repurposed for any reason. There's nowhere else I'd rather see it, she told me.

That Thanksgiving in Boston, my mother gave me the ring. Once I got home, I took it to a jeweler to pick out a necklace to go with it. My father had worn it continuously for forty-nine years—at work and at home, in the car and on public transit, while raking leaves and grilling hamburgers and taking out the trash. He had been twenty-five when my mother put it on him. He was seventy-four when she took it off. Life had grown on it, grown into it; for as long as I could remember, the grooves of the pattern had been charcoal, the surface a flat deep bronze. But while I was browsing, the jeweler polished it, and when he handed it back to me, my eyes filled with tears: it looked as it must have when my parents first saw it, the color of midmorning sunshine.

For months afterward, I kept the ring with its new necklace in my desk drawer, waiting for I'm not sure what—the right moment, the right occasion, the right mood. That February, C. and I both came down with one of those dreadful winter colds, the kind that makes you miserable in part by making you disgusting. We had low-grade fevers and deep racking coughs and seemingly endless quantities of mucus; when we woke up in the mornings, the sheets were clammy and our eyes were encrusted with microbial goop. By the third night, we felt too lousy to make dinner, or even remain upright at the table. Instead, we sat in bed, eating ramen, surrounded by used tissues and the empty capsule packages from daytime/nighttime cold meds. I felt exhausted and achy and unable to swallow and also, quite suddenly, overwhelmed by the desire to ask C. to marry me. Outside of early childhood, I had never wanted to be in someone's company when I was ill. But I wanted to be in C.'s company all the time, even when we were both objectively repellant. I looked at her and felt a wild flare of adoration and gratitude and tenderness and even, improbable and impracticable as it was under the circumstances, desire. In sickness and in health, I thought: here at last was someone I knew I would cherish through both. I had just enough wherewithal to look around and keep myself from blurting out the words.

Granted, I had never planned to go down on one knee in a rose garden in Paris; still, I realized, anything short of a trip to the landfill would be a more romantic way to propose than this. And so instead I touched her feverish cheek and blew my nose and, with difficulty, held my tongue.

I suppose it was partly the effort of doing so that caused me to propose when I did. Some weeks had passed. We were, at the time, in the middle of a top-to-bottom DIY renovation of our home, and that particular afternoon, we were upstairs in the guest room, laying new flooring. Eventually, C., who was planning to attend evening services, stripped out of her jeans and work shirt, went to take a shower, and emerged transformed, beautiful and a little bit solemn and dressed for church. I kissed her goodbye at the door and went back upstairs to inspect our progress. Almost half the floor was done; I looked at it and figured I could probably finish by the time she returned. I took a new batch of boards into the adjacent room, which we'd turned into a temporary woodshop, and trimmed them down to size. It took maybe three minutes. Then I walked them back into the guest room and set them down on the subfloor and in that exact moment it came to me that I must ask C. to marry me when she got home. The force of this feeling propelled me out of the room and into the shower. I scrubbed the grime and sawdust from my body, feeling clear and excited and nervous and ebullient, like something that had long been contained and was now on the point of release, a dove in a box or a horse at the post. Afterward I got dressed as if I, too, were going to church, and went downstairs to make dinner. We had pasta in the pantry, onions and tomatoes on the counter, fennel and feta cheese in the refrigerator; together, they became what I hope will be known forever in our family as proposal soup. I had just set the table and lit a candle when C. walked in the door, a cross of ashes on her forehead.

I admit, until that moment, the ecclesiastical calendar had been the furthest thing from my mind. I knew that C. had gone to church, obviously, but I hadn't for a moment stopped to think about why. Now, looking at her, I suddenly felt alarmed: however secular of a Jew I may be, I would not have proposed marriage on Yom Kippur. She, meanwhile, hadn't noticed anything unusual about me or about the evening—and why would she? I had simply showered after working on the floors, as she had done, and made us dinner, as I often do. We sat down to break her Lenten fast, and for the second time in a month I found myself wondering over a bowl of soup if I should put off asking her to marry me. Meanwhile, C. asked about the flooring and talked about her evening, and then told me a story about another Ash Wednesday service some years back, one that she herself had helped officiate: after the sermon, a little girl had come up to the altar with her mother, belatedly grasped the point of the occasion, and, just as C. bent to make the mark of the cross on her forehead, there in the solemn hush of the sanctuary, hollered at the top of her tiny lungs, "I don't want to die!"

Ashes to ashes, dust to dust. The candle flame bent double, then straightened up again. The world moves with our laughter, with our breath, with our grief, just not very much. The firelight fell on C. as in a Flemish painting, setting her loveliness against the dark. I had in my pocket a wedding ring that six months earlier had been on my father's hand. I did not want to die, either. I especially did not want to die without telling C. that I loved her, that I would always love her, that I wanted to marry her. I did not want to die without *being* married to her, for forty-nine or seventy-nine or preferably a thousand and ninety-nine years. Deathbeds, sickrooms, a smudge of ashes on her brow: I would wait forever, I realized, if I waited until suffering and sorrow were nowhere to be found. We had finished eating; I led her into the living room and sat her down beside me on the couch.

OF THE MILLION-SOME words in the English language, "and" is the third most common—three times as common as "I," four times as common as "you," trailing behind only "the" and the combined conjugations of the verb "to be." If you have spoken more than three or four sentences today, you have almost certainly used it; if you have gotten this far in this book, you have read it nearly two thousand times.

But if "and" is among the most everyday of words, it is also, in an understated way, one of the most existentially provocative. The world as described by other conjunctions seems to obey a set of specific, discernible rules: things precede each other or follow each other, preclude each other or cause each other. But the world as described by "and" is just an endless disorganized list. My mother and my father, C. and me, grief and love, life and death, yaks and harmonicas, playwrights and hay bales and polynomial equations, hurricanes and sweatshops and smallpox and Pop-Tarts, DNA and "Oh, Danny Boy" and Addis Ababa and the rings of Saturn and Zoroastrianism and clinical depression and Flanders Fields and Billie Holiday and the eight hundred and forty indigenous languages of Papua New Guinea— already we are confronting a chaotic abundance, and we have enumerated less than a paragraph's worth of the countless and-able things of the universe.

Like finding something or losing something, this quality of endless conjunction has the effect of making the world seem extraordinarily large and our own place in it vanishingly small. It also mimics a kind of imaginary primeval state of knowledge, as if everything in existence has been tossed down haphazardly in front us, leaving us to determine what relationships, if any, govern it all. One possible answer to that question was proposed by Elizabeth Bishop, who, in addition to her interest in losing things, was interested in the scale of the world and the problem of how to make sense of its wildly different parts. In "Over 2,000 Illustrations and a Complete Concordance," she moves from describing images in a Bible to describing images of the world as she journeys through it. Unlike the contents of the book, the contents of real life—in this case, a corpse, a jukebox, some goats, a British duchess, young Moroccan prostitutes—resist being brought into any kind of concordance. They are bound together only by the coincidence of existing at the same time, and by the fact of a traveler being there to witness them. That is Bishop's provocative suggestion: that no other, more orderly relationship exists among all the disparate stuff around us. Instead, life is made up of countless unrelated fragments, "Everything only connected by 'and' and 'and.'"

As it happens, there is a word for things that are "only connected by 'and' and 'and.'" That grammatical construction is known as polysyndeton, meaning "many bindings." It shows up frequently in the Old Testament—for instance, when God calls down a drought upon Jerusalem: "upon the land, and upon the mountains, and upon the corn, and upon the new wine, and upon the oil, and upon that which the ground bringeth forth, and upon men, and upon cattle, and upon all the labour of the hands." As you'll see if you read that example out loud, polysyndeton is an effective rhetorical device in part because of the long, slow, wave-form shape it gives to sentences. The effect is sometimes incantatory and sometimes ecstatic; in either of two directions, it conjures a sense of awe. Not by accident is there so much polysyndeton in the Bible.

And not by accident is the Bible the foil to the world in Bishop's poem. To the question of what binds together all of the stuff around us, it offers the opposite answer: a divinely ordained plan, with each element occupying its right and necessary place. Between these two poles—that nothing is meaningfully connected; that everything is meaningfully connected—lie plenty of other ways to make sense of existence. It is perfectly possible to believe in a creator God while holding that, outside of certain basic laws of nature, much of what appears to be deliberately connected is merely thrown together by chance. And it is perfectly possible to not believe in God at all, yet still feel that there are meaningful relations all around us—that everyone and everything is here for a reason, and that, in deep and important ways, we are all connected.

I myself hold this last belief: like a beautiful literary passage, we have many bindings. The ones that interest me most, however, are not necessarily intrinsic. They are created or inferred—the product, as it were, of Bishop's watchful traveler. Whatever you think about the supra-human organization of the cosmos, we ourselves organize it all the time, and the ability to do so is one of the most distinctive features of the human mind. It is why we can look at a night sky full of stars and see a bear and a cross and a warrior with his sword, and it is why we can recognize the influence of *Oedipus Rex* on *Hamlet,* and it is why we know that ostriches are distantly related to dinosaurs. More generally, it is how we wrest order from confusion, transforming life's boundless list into something more like a story, full of structure, information, and meaning. Granted, this ability is not without drawbacks; it is also why we leap to conclusions and why we are so susceptible to conspiracy theories. Still, it is almost impossible to overstate how emotionally, ethically, and intellectually impaired we would be if we could not perceive connections among seemingly dissimilar things.

To begin with, this ability is a fundamental part of how we think—so fundamental that some people believe it *is* how we think. The philosopher David Hume, for one, held that all ideas emerge from conjunction, from linking one known component of the world to another. "All this creative power of the mind amounts to no more than the faculty of compounding, transposing, augmenting, or diminishing the materials afforded us by the senses and experience," he wrote in *An Enquiry Concerning Human Understanding.* "When we think of a golden mountain, we only join two consistent ideas, *gold* and *mountain,* with which we were formerly acquainted." One way to think new thoughts, then, is to make, quite literally, new connections. The nonsense poet Gelett Burgess had never seen a purple cow, but he had seen purple and he had seen a cow, and by combining them he thought up something wholly original. So, too, with other, more important conjunctions: not just *women* and *children* but *women* and *suffrage;* not just *human* and *animal* but *human* and *rights.* In the math of the mind, in other words, the most powerful operation might be simple addition. "Connect the dots," we tell people when we want them to understand something; comprehension emerges when we can see the links between things.

But something else emerges under those conditions, too. If conjunction lies close to the origins of thought, as Hume believed, it also lies close to the origins of morality. The more closely we believe ourselves to be connected to other people, the more likely we are to hold ourselves at least partly responsible for their well-being. As our current turbulent era has made exceptionally clear, the actions we take or do not take—in the face of pandemics, prejudice, authoritarianism, resource use, climate change—affect even strangers, even those who live far away from us, sometimes even those who are not yet living at all. It is easy to ignore all those other people, to regard ourselves as linked only to our own family and community. Yet our moral power, like our intellectual power, comes from asserting connections that have previously been invisible or overlooked.

That is a solemn reason to nurture our sense of connection; and yet the more densely we are tied to others, the happier we are. Many of us have occasionally felt the world to be as Bishop describes it in her poem: disconnected, fragmentary, devoid of logic and meaning. And many of us have occasionally felt ourselves to be disconnected as well—felt that, whatever the state of the world, we stand apart from its workings, unable to muster interest in doing anything or, alternatively, convinced that nothing we do will matter. These are not pleasant feelings. To be disconnected is to be lonely, indifferent, estranged—in one way or another, cut off from the rest of humanity. As a psychological state, it is at best distressing and at worst dangerous, both for the people experiencing it and for those around them. One famous description of hell holds that it is a place where "nothing connects with nothing," suggesting that the absence of attachment to the rest of the world is both an abdication of goodness and a form of suffering. By contrast, the more deeply connected we feel, the more fulfilling we typically find our lives.

These emotional and intellectual powers of conjunction are themselves conjoined in the domain of romance, since every experience of falling in love is both a bid for happiness and an act of imagining a new connection into being. Schoolkids in the throes of their first crush write "SH + JB" or "JM + MF" over and over in their notebooks (that plus sign, incidentally, having most likely evolved as a simplified form of the ampersand). It doesn't matter if JB is uninterested and MF barely knows who JM is. In linking themselves to someone else, those infatuated kids both reflect an emotional reality and try to will into being a bond that did not previously exist.

Wonderfully, this sometimes works. Like purple cows and golden mountains, people can become linked by connections that emerge out of nowhere and gradually turn robust and enduring. That is how, over time, in their own hearts and to their friends and family, Margot and Isaac became *Margot and Isaac,* and Bill and Sandy became *Bill and Sandy.* And so, too, with C. and me: eventually, we could no longer imagine ourselves without that *and* between us.

HERE IS WHAT happened, unbeknownst to the two of us, just before our wedding began. While we were standing outside on the porch of a bed-and-breakfast, gazing now at each other and now at the lovely confluence of land and water and sky, happier than ever before in our lives and better dressed; while our friends and relatives were starting to take their seats in the rows of chairs set up a short distance down the point from where we stood; while the last of the little kids were corralled by their parents up toward those chairs and away from the temptations of hammock and Frisbee and water and dock; while our officiant was taking a final moment to look over her notes; while my niece was touching the soft curve of the petals in the basket of flowers she carried—it was while all this was happening that every cellphone in every shoulder bag and suit pocket of our assembled guests simultaneously blared out, in the most urgent tones imaginable, a tornado warning.

The sound wafted away from C. and me over the water. We had no idea that anything out of the ordinary was happening, apart from the obviously out-of-the-ordinary thing that was happening for us that day. Even if we had heard the warning, it would have seemed, as it did to our guests, impossible to believe. The sky that afternoon had the high, mild look of early summer, untroubled by clouds, three shades lighter than the cobalt water of the bay. The sun was shining forth like an irrepressible good mood, filling the cup of every tulip and daffodil, gilding the wheat-like tips of the marsh grass, making shifting little lakes of shade beneath the trees. The lightest of breezes ruffled the air; my wedding vows, set down upon a table, would not have blown away. The bay was lapping placidly against the rocks just beyond the little bower where soon we would be married. It was, in short, the kind of day that everyone dreams of for their wedding.

By then, C. and I had been dreaming of it from the moment on that Ash Wednesday evening when she had said yes. For much of the intervening time, though, we had *only* been dreaming of it: talking, not idly but in the abstract, about what kind of wedding we wanted to have. Virtually the only thing I was clear on from the beginning was that I didn't want to elope, even though several friends of ours had done so, for understandable and in many ways admirable reasons. The fact that it was by far the most affordable option made it both economically and ethically appealing; the subsequent conversations C. and I had about weddings and resources, financial and otherwise, could fill the Talmud. This is a common kind of "and": you want a lovely wedding in a beautiful place filled with all the people you love and delicious things to eat and drink, and you also want to spend your money wisely and responsibly and in ways that reflect your values and won't make you go broke, and it would be nice if none of these goals were ever in conflict but, inevitably, they often are. Needless to say, this problem—of wanting multiple incompatible things, of feeling torn between our desires and our convictions—neither begins nor ends with nuptials.

But I had two overriding feelings that made a quick trip to the courthouse impossible, one brought about by grief, the other by love. On the day I proposed, my father's memorial service was six months in the past, but I still sometimes felt like I was slumped in a chair in its exhausting aftermath, not yet changed out of my brand-new black suit. Life, I understood acutely, would give us plenty of reasons to come together in sorrow. And so it seemed to me incumbent on us to create reasons to come together in joy, as a gift to ourselves, our families, our friends, and, in some strange way, to the world itself, to its precarious balance of shining and terrible.

The other feeling was more basic, yet more surprising to me. I am neither a personal nor a political cynic about weddings, and I have generally experienced those I've attended as somewhere on a scale from fun to beautiful. But I hadn't been the kind of little girl who dreams about the one she'll someday have, and even the loneliest stretches of my adulthood hadn't inspired in me any fantasies about one day standing up and declaring my abiding love for someone in front of all my family and friends. In my entire life, only C. had ever made me want to do that, and by the time we were discussing what to do about a wedding, everyone I was close to already knew how much I adored her. Yet I found myself wanting to pull them into the circle of my gladness, to rejoice with them as she and I made fast the "and" between us.

So we would get married, we decided, the conventional way, in front of those who had helped shape us and filled our lives with joy. By the time we worked that out, however, together with various other emotional, philosophical, and practical priorities, and finally got around to planning the actual wedding, we discovered that we were extremely late in doing so. (At one point, C.'s younger sister, meaning to be helpful, gave us some kind of bridal-magazine timeline for planning a wedding. As I recall, we had already missed the first deadline by a year.) There was the matter of where and when; of what to eat and drink; of what to do about music, since we both love to dance; of what to do in the event of rain. In an ideal world, we would have gotten married in the backyard of our own home, but we were still in the middle of renovating it—a process that, for most of its duration, looks indistinguishable from demolishing it. Committing ourselves to finishing the job in time for the wedding we were simultaneously scrambling to plan was, we realized in a moment of sanity, insane.

At any event, all those dire warnings turned out to be unnecessary; once we finally began planning, everything fell into place with affirming speed. C.'s father, that finder par excellence, told us about a spot he'd heard about down at the tip of an island in the bay, and as soon as we saw it, we knew it was the place. C. herself was friends with a caterer she had worked for all through high school and on college breaks, and he had urged her many times in the subsequent years to call him the moment she decided to get married. When she did, though, he groaned and gave us the you're-awfully-late speech, then told her that he was booked for the next fourteen months, minus one weekend in May, for which he was waiting to hear back on a bid. We hung up and turned our minds to Plan B. Ten minutes later, he called back. He'd pulled the bid, he said; if we could do that weekend, he'd be there.

That solved two problems: the food and the date. We made the invitations ourselves, out of card stock and rubber cement and beautiful old postage stamps, thanks to C.'s mother, the letter carrier, who bought us a batch at a yard sale. The flowers came to us courtesy of C.'s younger sister, who knew of a farmer in their hometown who grew acres of wildflowers. C.'s older sister, a beer and wine connoisseur, said she'd handle the drinks. An old friend and professional baker who had furnished dessert for every family celebration beginning with C.'s seventh birthday (and carrying on through the acquiring of puppies, the winning of farm-queen pageants, miscellaneous parties, high school graduations, college acceptances, new jobs, parental anniversaries, and recoveries from various illnesses and injuries—at a conservative estimate, some hundred and fifty confections in total) made our wedding cake.

It had all felt charmed at every stage, and never more so than on that lovely day in May. Still, if it had occurred to us to pause in our happiness to feel relief, I suppose we would have done so, because we had each had our share of concerns about the wedding in the months leading up to it. I had never for a moment forgotten that my father wouldn't be there—that a ragged edge would gape open in the place where the family I was forming met the family that formed me—and I worried that grief in its most overwhelming incarnation would come find me that day. C. was spared that anxiety but harbored another I had never had to face. Some years earlier, at the wedding of one of her cousins, she had looked around at her relatives and wondered how many of them would show up if she got married. Her immediate family loved her and would always be at her side, she knew, and, from the beginning, they had been wonderful to me. But she was from the kind of place that made the comparatively rapid and widespread acceptance of same-sex couples seem distant, a wave in the culture that had not yet reached its farthest shores, and that day at her cousin's wedding, she had felt a steep and unexpected sadness. She had grown up close to her many aunts and uncles and cousins, hunting and fishing and going on camping trips with them, traipsing from one house to another for birthdays and crab feasts and another round of food on Christmas Day. And she is at home among them in a way that goes deeper than every other home she has in the world. The first time I met a wide swath of them, at a retirement party for one of her aunts, I watched her, at ease and full of laughter, and thought about what a giddy relief it had been, in the years when I lived abroad, to meet a compatriot and spend an evening speaking English. For C., there was no way to think about marrying me without confronting the painful likelihood that some of the people she loved most in the world might choose not to be there.

If you ever want to have a larger wedding than you anticipated, try underestimating your extended family. We invited them, hopefully and doubtfully; to a person, they came. That day, when the ceremony was minutes from starting, they were all already settled and beaming in their chairs. Behind them, standing next to C. on the porch, I felt almost unable to contain my emotions, as if more of them had showed up than expected, too. Falling in love, getting married, having children, grieving, dying: how commonplace all of life's grand transitions are in the abstract, how overwhelming when they happen to you. C. walked down the aisle first, between her father and her mother, then turned around alone to face me, framed against a backdrop of flowers and trees and water and sky. It was Main Street, inverted and completed; there she was waiting for me, in all of her remarkable specificity, and there I was, about to marry her.

There was, in the end, nothing to worry about, everything to celebrate. I met one of C.'s more conservative uncles for the first time that day, a giant of a man with a beard like Grizzly Adams and a build like Stonehenge; one of my fondest memories from the entire wedding is how he swept me up into a bear hug that could have lifted off the ground an actual bear. I have adored him ever since (even after the following Fourth of July, when he accidentally almost hit me with a firecracker that must have been illegal in forty-one states), and I like to think the feeling is mutual. As for my father, his loss was palpable to me throughout, but only in the way that the moon is sometimes visible by day: faint and strangely beautiful, there only because it is always there.

It was from having a wedding that I learned another reason to do so, one that I could not have anticipated beforehand. I don't know how often, if ever, our families will have occasion to come together like that again. But I am glad they did so at least once, to honor the fact that, in the historical record, they have now been brought together permanently. Love is not just the private "&" that joins one person to another, whether scribbled in notebooks or printed on wedding invitations. It is also the genealogical "and," the kind that signifies the confluence of families and the accumulation of generations. Like grief, love rearranges existing relationships: I am bound now to C.'s entire lineage and she to mine, and they are bound to each other in perpetuity.

That union, like so many others, is made richer and more wonderful for all the differences it spans. "Glory be to God for dappled things," Gerard Manley Hopkins wrote in a poem of praise for all the coupled contrasts of the world, for all things "swift, slow; sweet, sour; adazzle, dim." And God knows, we were a dappled bunch that day—Jewish and Christian, atheist and devout, rural and urban, conservative and progressive, straight and queer. I know that to some of our guests, our wedding must have felt traditional, for reasons that began with its very existence and continued on from there: the aisle to walk down, the rings to exchange, the tent under which we ate dinner, the general if approximate hewing to the usual order of things. And I know that to others, it must have felt radical, for reasons that also began with its very existence and continued on from there: no gifts, no bridal shower, no rehearsal dinner, no wedding dress, no member of the clergy to marry us, a series of readings that would not have been out of place in a graduate seminar. But truly, who, on such an occasion, could possibly care? We read from the Bible, broke a glass, said grace before the meal, were lifted up laughing in our chairs to dance the hora; outside of wishing my father had been there, I can't imagine a single thing I would change about that day.

Including this: after the ceremony, after the dinner, after the toasts, after dessert, after night had long since fallen and half the party was sitting talking and the other half was on the dance floor, I looked out into the darkness and saw, way down low along the horizon, a towering bank of clouds turn swiftly, briefly orange. I appreciated the distance the storm was keeping, as well as its tactful timing, and turned back to the party. Twenty minutes later it hit, with a wallop of thunder so loud I thought at first one of the nearby walnut trees had come crashing to the ground. The rain arrived immediately and drastically, rushing at us sideways like white water over the prow of a ship. An admirably sane minority bolted immediately for the indoors. The rest of us stayed for a while, half-protected and doubtless half-endangered by the tent, watching with a kind of mesmerized exultant glee as, all around our three-hundred-degree panorama, lightning branched down the sky and lit up the bay. After a few minutes of this I went up to C.'s friend the caterer, who was by then on the dance floor, and who also by then had worked two decades' worth of events on the water. Shouting to be heard over the music and the storm, I asked him if the most wonderful day of my life was about to end in the sudden and horrible death of everyone I loved most in the world. "I

don't know," he shouted back, which was equivocal enough
for me. But just as I was starting to round up the guests to
herd them inside, a particularly dramatic bolt of lightning
turned the whole world white and, as one, we shot out of
the tent and, dress shoes squelching and sinking into the
grass, raced for the covered porch.

No tornado touched down on the Eastern Shore that
night, but seldom in my life have I experienced such an epic
storm. I would not have thought to request it, if it had been
in my power to design down to the level of meteorology the
events of my wedding, but I can't imagine a better ending to
our lovely sunny day. A few people headed off to bed; the
rest of us bundled into the chairs and couches on the porch,
talking and laughing and snacking on a tin of cookies that
someone had produced out of nowhere, all the while watching the spellbinding sky. I remember in particular my mother
sitting there among us, looking wet and radiant and lively
enough to stay up with us until two in the morning, which
she did.

But long before that, one last unexpected thing trans-
pired. At ten minutes to midnight, C., who seldom forgets
anything, shot upright out of her chair. What she had remembered, all of a sudden, was the marriage license, which,
in the happy tumult of the day, we had completely forgotten
to sign. In retrospect, I suppose we could have just let it go
and backdated it the next day, but somehow in the moment
that seemed like the wrong way to start our married life,
and so I went upstairs and roused from her imminent slum-
ber the jet-lagged British friend who had served as our officiant.

We have, by design, no video of our actual wedding ceremony, but someone got out a phone and made a recording

of our impromptu second one. In it, I am sitting in C.'s lap as our officiant, in pajamas and high spirits, signs us with a grand eleventh-hour flourish into marriage. All around us, our family and friends raise another round of drinks, and C. pulls me in for a kiss. Then a bolt of lightning switch-backs down the sky behind us, and for a moment, all you can hear is laughter, and all you can see is light.

IT IS so rare, a day like that—a day of ongoing, unadulter-ated, self-evident joy. I don't mean that, among emotions, joy is particularly ephemeral; I mean that it is unusual to experience any emotion all on its own for a sustained length of time. Physical sensations, even those that afflict a com-paratively healthy body, can be relentless. A sufficiently bad toothache or any other persistent pain can dominate your every waking moment. But even the strongest sentiments are intermittent and inconstant, forever obliged to share the stage with other members of emotion's ensemble cast—grief with gratitude, anger with boredom, happiness with irritation, frustration with amusement, and on and on, in endless permutations.

Most of us instinctively resent this intermingling. When we are happy, we want to be wholly happy, not also missing our father or worried about work or infuriated by the awful customer service at the phone company. That appetite for contentment makes perfect sense—but we often long to ex-perience our disagreeable feelings uninterrupted as well. In part, that's because misery has a kind of inertia to it; there is something about a bad mood that wants, perversely, to persist. I have felt, at various low points in my life, that I did not want to venture out to a social event because I would have to pretend to be happy, forgetting the very real possibility that, once there, I would actually *be* happy—or, perhaps more accurately, believing that I did not want to feel better. Worse, I have sometimes persevered in a pointless argument simply because I was in the kind of sour mood that would rather fight than be improved. This kind of emotional intransigence is common. Anger wants only to be angry (levity is deadly to it, as is compassion; accordingly, it resists them both); boredom rejects as boring everything that might vanquish it; loneliness wants only to be left alone; and grief, as I noted earlier, is so terrified of betraying itself that it wants only to grieve.

Yet this tendency toward inertia is not the only reason we long for undiluted emotion. That yearning also has to do with a mistaken sense of how we are supposed to experience the most important aspects of our lives. We have a notion of what love is, a bright, clear stream of joy flowing continuously through a sunlit valley, and we have a notion of what grief is, a dreadful crack and fall, as of some great limb coming down, bringing the soul it strikes to its knees. Those ideas do describe some part of each experience, but they don't capture what it really means to be in love or to be bereft. Plenty of other feelings crowd in, some of them in the same general register. Love really is that clear and constant stream, but it is also desire and tenderness and admiration and gratitude. And grief really is that terrible fracture, but, as I learned after my father died, it is also anxiety and irritability and yearning.

Moreover, plenty of feelings in other registers characterize each experience as well. It is virtually impossible to mourn without sometimes feeling nothing and sometimes feeling the "wrong" thing—some mood or emotion wholly unsuited to our idea of grief. To be bereft is to be furious at total strangers one day and unbearably moved by them the next; it is to feel, depending on the loss or the moment, bleak amusement and covert resentment and a current of relief and powerful regret. And we love as we mourn, with wildly variegated, equally sincere emotions. In addition to everything lofty and lusty, love is also being hurt when your wife is brusque with you or annoyed when you realize that your husband has walked past the cat vomit all day without cleaning it up; it is alternately intervening and forbearing when your beloved bites her nails, and listening patiently as your partner vents at length about his boss when you really just want to get back to reading your book. There is no enduring love on the planet, nor ever has been, that isn't characterized by these crisscrossing moods. "Whoever supposes," Montaigne once wrote, "to see me look sometimes coldly, sometimes lovingly, on my wife, that either look is feigned, is a fool."

We think of all these other emotions as supernumerary, as obscuring or even defiling the real thing. But there is no real thing—or, rather, taken together, this grab bag of reactions *is* the real thing. Love is the totality of ways you feel while in love; grief is the totality of ways you feel while grieving. Everything else is just an abstraction, a stream or a tree limb in the mind. "One never meets just Cancer, or War, or Unhappiness (or Happiness)," C. S. Lewis wrote in *A Grief Observed*. "One only meets each hour or moment that comes." And whether you are living through happiness or cancer, the hours change and change. We all have, as Lewis wrote, "many bad spots in our best times, many good ones in our worst."

I know of no clearer example of this in my own life than the reception that followed my father's memorial service—which, despite the loss that occasioned it, ranks as one of the greatest parties I have ever attended. The service itself felt more or less as I would have expected, somber and loving and elegiac. But the get-together afterward, in an old friend's front yard on a beautiful autumn evening, just down the street from that house where I grew up, was something else entirely. I doubt I would have believed it if someone had told me so beforehand, but it was incredibly fun. I love the people who loved my father, and never more so than that night; just at the moment the world seemed emptiest, they replenished it, bringing us their laughter and their stories and their matter-of-fact kindness, giving it back its golden edge. I remember looking around at all of them toward the end of the evening, full of gratitude and chocolate cake—after weeks of barely being able to eat, I had found myself suddenly famished—and thinking, not at all mournfully, about how much my father would have loved to be there. That moment is as inseparable from my experience of grieving him as the one when I watched a nurse disconnect all the monitors and IVs on the day we decided that the time had come to let him die.

Anyone who has ever been bereft understands the importance of the kind of gladness I felt that evening. It diverts, for a moment, the clear stream to the devastated clearing; it lifts our eyes to some light terribly but, as it reminds us, not impossibly distant. Still, the price we pay for this changeability of emotion is steep: sometimes, sadness derails our joy instead. I know this, because I have felt the light shift suddenly not only on my darkest days but on my brightest ones, too. Some months after C. and I got married, we finally sat down to look through all the photographs from our wedding. We were in the middle of delightedly reexperiencing it when we came upon one of my mother and me, standing side by side on the waterfront, beaming. It is a beautiful picture, and the elation in both of us is evident. But looking at it after the fact, all I could see was the vast expanse of the Chesapeake Bay on my other side, a wide blue emptiness where my father should have been. It was the starkest possible representation of the way that grief had reorganized my family; his absence was so obvious that he almost seemed to have been edited out of the picture. I felt a sudden and excruciating double anguish—for how much I missed my father, and for how much my father, gone at that point for under two years, had already missed.

That picture has been on the wall beside me the whole time I have been writing this book. After the shock of first seeing it wore off, I came to love it very much, partly for the way it makes my loss visible and beautiful—it feels like the closest thing I have to a picture of my father at my wedding—but chiefly because, in a single image, it honors my joy together with my grief. That seems right to me. Life, too, goes by contraries: it is by turns crushing and restorative, busy and boring, awful and absurd and comic and uplifting. We can't get away from this constant amalgamation of feeling, can't strain out the ostensible impurities in pursuit of some imaginary essence, and we shouldn't want to if we could. The world in all its complexity calls on us to respond in kind, so that to be conflicted is not to be adulterated; it is to be complete.

———

Last night i fell asleep before C., curled up against her
back while she stayed awake for a while, reading. I have the
faintest memory of her body stretching briefly away from
mine as she reached to turn out the light, and then it was
morning. We had reversed positions; I was facing the wall
and she was wrapped around me, her hand holding mine.
One of our cats, the impossibly affectionate one, had
crawled into our intertwined arms and made himself a
home there, purring away contentedly beside me. Some
years ago, in the course of doing research for an article I was
writing, I learned that organisms that actively seek out
physical contact are described by scientists as thigmotactic.
Our cat is exceedingly thigmotactic. So, with respect to each
other, are we. "Close close all night / the lovers keep. / They
turn together / in their sleep," Elizabeth Bishop once wrote,
in the opening lines of a silly, smitten, charming little poem
that she never published, and that nicely characterizes C.
and me at night. Who is to say where love ends and biology
begins, or how they shape each other, or how much our cat's
feelings and motivations do and do not differ from our own?
I only know that it is very rare that C. and I ever wake up
apart from each other in the morning.

   This particular morning, we woke up in our own bed,
here in Maryland. We no longer travel as much as we used
to, and so our schedule has become far more predictable;
entire months go by where we scarcely stray from home.
Today, we worked for a while in the office we share, and then
C. migrated to the dining room table, and then we both
went upstairs, to a room with a couch big enough for both
of us and a little schoolhouse desk set in an alcove. The cats
followed us from room to room, the thigmotactic one from

lap to lap. In the afternoon we took a break and went out to inspect the waning late-September status of our vegetable garden and stroll along an old split-rail fence that C.'s father helped us rebuild when we first moved in. Every spring since then, we have sown a swath of wildflowers alongside it, a lavish, ever-changing, summer-long bouquet. By this time of the year, they are almost as tall as we are and starting to go to seed, but we still like to walk the length of them to see what we can see—a late, bright riot of cosmos; the last of the dusky blue cornflowers; fat, pollen-packed fingers of goldenrod; a smattering of bright pink zinnias, each one as round and closely petaled as an old-fashioned lady's swim cap. In August so many butterflies find their way to the flowers that we sometimes see two and three on a single stalk; now those are gone, but grasshoppers catapult out of our way by the dozen as we walk, and when we return along the little pond out back, we hear at every step the startled yelp and plop of bullfrogs leaping in.

"I have often thought," C.'s father, Bill, once told me, "that for a completely average person, I have lived a remarkable life." He had grown up without indoor plumbing and lived to carry a cellphone around in his pocket, its ringtone set to emergency-alert volume to be heard over his tractor; he had married the love of his life and raised three wonderful children; he had worked as a farmer, a grocery-store clerk, a custodian, and a caretaker all his days, yet he had met four presidents—one who gave a speech on the Eastern Shore, two who employed his oldest daughter, one who spoke at C.'s college graduation; he had found, against staggering odds, a falling star. I knew what he meant, and I knew that he would have felt the same even if he had never met so much as a mayor and never even seen a meteorite.

Because I, too, feel that way: that my days are exceptional even when they are ordinary, that existence does not need to show us any of its more famous or spectacular wonders to fill us with amazement. We live remarkable lives because life itself is remarkable, a fact that is impossible not to notice if only suffering leaves us alone for long enough.

Lately I have found this everyday remarkableness almost overwhelming. As I said, I've never been much for stoicism, but these last few years, I have been even more susceptible than usual to emotion—or, rather, to one emotion in particular. As far as I know, it has no name in our language, although it is close to what the Portuguese call *saudade* and the Japanese call *mono no aware*. It is the feeling of registering, on the basis of some slight exposure, our existential condition: how lovely life is, and how fragile, and how fleeting. Although this feeling is partly a response to our place in the universe, it is not quite the same as awe, because it has too much of the everyday in it, and too much sorrow, too. For the same reason, it is also not the feeling the Romantics identified as the sublime—a mingling of admiration and dread, evoked by the vast impersonal grandeur of the physical world. This feeling I am talking about has none of that splendor or terror in it. It is made up, instead, of gratitude, longing, and a note I can only call anticipatory grief. Among English words, its nearest kin might be "bittersweet," a translation of the Greek term Sappho coined to describe the experience of falling in love; it was she who first and forever soldered love's joy to love's suffering. But while "bittersweet" accurately captures the mingling of happiness and sadness in this feeling, its intimate origin means that it lacks the necessary world-facing aspect, the sense of the scale of the problem: all that we have, we will someday lose. Of every kind of "and" that we experience, I find this one the most acute—the awareness that our love, in all its many forms, is bound inseparably to our grief.

It is a measure of how porous I am at present that this feeling can be provoked in me by almost anything: basic human decency, extraordinary acts of courage, works of art that remind me of the inexplicable brilliance of our species. I have felt it on a summer night after accidentally killing a firefly, which left a luminous, upsetting stain on our bedroom wall; and on a November evening after finding a six-week-old kitten outside in the pouring rain, full of need and life, howling for help like something fifty times its size; and rising up in me out of nowhere amid the past-midnight laughter of good friends, with whom C. and I had lingered for hours after dinner, the candles long since reduced to wax glaciers, the wine to stained-glass crescents on the bottom of each glass. It has come over me indoors and out, in broad daylight and in darkness, alone and in company, so that I have to stay quiet for a moment or briefly turn my face away.

I don't think this feeling I am describing is the same as sentimentality, the emotion produced by tearjerker movies and corny commercials and sappy, circle-of-life country songs. That word implies an excess of emotion, typically provoked through manipulative means, but neither accusation applies in this case. Nothing could be less manipulative than the things that fill me with this tender, mournful feeling; they are best summed up as the world just being the world. And as for excess—well, how are we supposed to feel about the fact that we will eventually lose everything we love, including our own lives? In the face of a fact like that, what emotion could possibly count as disproportionate?

If anything, I am amazed that we aren't all overcome

more often by this mingled sense of gratitude and grief. And it makes sense to me that I have grown so susceptible to it after meeting C. and losing my father. In quick succession, I found one foundational love and lost another, and ever since, both the wonder and the fragility of life have been exceptionally present to me. I have put off mentioning it so far, but this is one of the most significant and difficult aspects of love, romantic and otherwise: it is terribly vulnerable to forces outside our control, and therefore terribly frightening. The corollary to "Now has your bliss appeared" is "Now, at any moment, it may vanish."

What gives this fear its awful force is that, unlike plenty of others that trouble us from time to time, it will someday come true. There is no "if" about whether you will lose your loved ones; there is only the how and the when. To those of us with active imaginations, such questions are a torment. "Who shall reach the end of his days and who shall not?" asks the Unetaneh Tokef, that eerie and lovely liturgical poem that Jews recite on the Day of Atonement. And when we do each reach our end, "who by sword and who by wild beast, who by famine and who by thirst, who by earthquake and who by plague, who by strangulation and who by stoning?" Those lines are evocative but incomplete, and it is easy to lie awake at night adding our own verses. Who by cancer and who by car accident? Who by heart attack and who by stroke? Who by firearm and who by flu and who by falling?

That list goes on and on, long and strange and sad enough to account for even the most shocking demise. So omnipresent and protean is death that there is, as Montaigne wrote, "no place from which it may not come to us," so that we "turn our heads constantly this way and that as in a suspicious country." Perhaps we will be among the fortunate, and all that vigilance will turn out to have been unnecessary; perhaps our loved ones will die peacefully, in old age, surrounded by their children and grandchildren. But what a cruelty that love, which wants only to tend and protect, should ultimately be so powerless to do so, that we must relegate to fate the most important thing in our lives, the well-being of those we hold dearest. To be happy is to have a lot of hap, that archaic word for luck: our joy, our bliss, is left terrifyingly up to chance.

It may be, of course, that I am unusually troubled by this problem. One of the difficulties of writing about one's own emotional life is that it is impossible to know how representative it is—how much it overlaps with or diverges from everyone else's inmost experience. Some people, I am sure, are spared by their psychology or their cosmology from worrying all that much about their loved ones. But I myself have always possessed a catastrophic what-if machine. Even as a very young child, I would lie awake in my bedroom on nights when my parents left my sister and me home with a babysitter, my mind full of drunk drivers and dark alleys and freak accidents, my fear relieved only by the sound of their car hitting the gravelly base of our driveway.

Over the years, I have grown more rational and better at self-soothing but at heart no less afraid, and falling in love has only exacerbated the problem. All my endless imaginary tragedies befall C. now, and when she is out somewhere without me, the car I listen for in the dark is hers. For that matter, even having her safely home beside me cannot always ease my fears. Sometimes, I rest my head against her chest and listen—as I suppose all lovers have done from time immemorial—to the beating of her heart, and although I cherish the feel of her body and the sense of taking refuge there so near the core of her, it never fails to worry me a little. C. has a naturally rapid heart rate, much as she has a breakneck metabolism and can bound through a busy day on absurdly little sleep, and I sometimes worry that all this means that she is burning her brilliant candle too quickly— that someday far too soon, she will leave me alone in an unbanishable darkness.

Whether or not that comes to pass, however, the larger issue remains. We will each die, C. and I, and in addition to the how and the when, we are now both afflicted with the lovers' haunting question of which one of us will do so first. I imagine that many spouses have made each other un-keepable promises, have talked, as C. and I have done, about dying together in very old age in our sleep: entering death as we have entered almost every night and morning of our shared life, holding each other close, grateful and at peace.

Has any couple in the history of the world been so lucky? Perhaps one or two. But the odds are grievously against us. In all likelihood, one of us will leave the other alone in bed at night, alone on waking up to face the day: me, if we go by actuarial tables, because I am older; C., if we go by premo-nitions, because she had one, when she was a little girl, about dying young—a story I wish she had never told me, because now and then it fills me with a dread as huge and cold as the ocean. I do not want to die—it is impossible to overstate how true that is—but I would rather face my own death than survive hers. I cannot imagine that I will ever stop feeling this way, even if I am lucky and my fears for C. prove as premature as my childhood ones for my parents, and we are still tending our wildflowers together half a cen-tury hence. Yet even in that case I know how little balm, once the time comes, all that time will be. I have never forgotten a heartbreaking line in a letter I once received: "How fortunate I have been—and yet I wanted it to last longer." That was from my great-uncle, widowed after sixty-two years.

If anything, like all shadows, this one that trails behind love grows longer later in the day. When I was a child, death seemed like a contingency, an emergency, even though I understood in the abstract that it would come for all of us eventually. But after my father died I began to feel its inevitability, and I know that it will only grow more present with each passing year. We find things and lose things at all stages of life, but the overall distribution shifts over time, and loss strikes both more often and with more devastating intimacy as we age. And so the kind of difficulties we face shift as we grow older, too. The first problem that love presents us with is how to find it. But the most enduring problem of love, which is also the most enduring problem of life, is how to live with the fact that we will lose it.

SOMETHING LIKE AN answer to that question came to me on the most recent anniversary of my father's death. I had woken up early that day, into an ebbing darkness, with the unsettled feeling that there was something I should be doing. I recognized it right away—the feeling, I mean. It was the disquiet that anniversary always brings me, a sense of aimlessness brought about by having no good way to commemorate the occasion. Other than burning a yahrzeit candle, as Jews do on days of remembrance, I have never really known how to honor the steady accretion of years without my father. The conventional options, such as they are, are unavailable; because we donated his body to a medical school, there is no grave to visit, no place to return to where we scattered his ashes. C., who grew up (as I did not) with a tradition of regularly visiting the cemeteries where her relatives are buried, asked me, not long after he died, if I would like to have a stone of some kind carved for him and set out on our property where I could sit with it when I chose. At the time, I joked that I was pretty sure my father would rather spend the rest of eternity inside on a bookshelf; but either way, I never did have any kind of memorial made. Nor did I ever devise any strategy for recognizing occasions like the day of his birth and the day of his death, even though it has always seemed to me important and right to do so.

And so that morning when I woke up out of sorts and unsure of what to do, I delegated the problem to C., who took me for a walk in our local arboretum. We followed a looping trail through woodlands and meadows, past native sassafras and mountain laurel and shining sumac and a pasture full of goats, until we returned to the place where we had started, a little Monet-like pond with a wooden bridge across its middle. It was a beautiful September day, breezy and warm, and we stood there together for over an hour, leaning side by side against the railing, just watching: as two turtles sunned themselves on a half-submerged log, as a hummingbird swooped in to hover beside the long trumpet of a flowering vine, as a coot went for a splashy little swim, as a heron eased itself with impossible patience perhaps six inches eastward in sixty minutes, as a tapestry of sage-green algae shifted slow as light around the water.

I had had a lousy week leading up to that anniversary, a week of feeling, as I did shortly after my father died, low-level sick and stupidly clumsy and more emotional and irritable than usual—the bereft heart being as attuned to seasons as a migratory bird, and capable of registering, in ways both remarkable and annoying, the calendrical return of grief. But there in the arboretum with C., I felt at peace, and even content, in the adult way that contentment can coexist with whole histories of sorrow and distress—and indeed almost presupposes them, since it suggests an acceptance of life as it is. I didn't miss my father more that day than any other, and, as usual, I didn't feel his presence, either. But I was happy to slow time down for a spell there by the side of the pond, to do nothing at all for part of an afternoon but look at that dapple-green view. Since I could no longer sit with my father, it was good, on that day, to sit for a while with the world.

So much had happened in it since he had died. To begin with, a sobering number of other people had died, too, even before the devastation of the coronavirus, and even in the small compass of our own lives—friends of friends, gone in a month from lung cancer; parents of friends, gone overnight. So many babies had been born that each winter the mantel where we set our holiday cards looked like the cheerful bulletin board in the office of a busy obstetrician. We had celebrated with other couples as they got married; we had driven up to New York to help with the packing and unpacking and the buying of dishes and trash cans and bath mats after a close friend—the one whose wedding C. had attended the day before our first date—got divorced. When my mother needed a heart valve replaced, we had returned to the Cleveland Clinic, where a saturating bleakness immediately settled into me; I felt ten thousand years old, and felt like I had spent nine thousand and ninety-nine of them there in the hospital. Everything about the experience was dispiritingly familiar, except that two days later, my mother, looking healthy and happy and in no particular need of assistance, did what my father had not done and came back home.

It is true what people so often tell you in the face of hardship or heartache: life goes on. I have always liked that expression, hackneyed though it may be, for its refusal of easy consolation, for everything that it declines to say. It does not promise an end to pain, like "time heals all wounds" and "this too shall pass." It does not have the clean-slate undertones of "tomorrow is another day." It says only that things—good things, bad things, thing-things; it does not specify—will not stop happening. That is not so much a reassurance as a reminder: you will not just get to sit there for as long as you want, drinking your sorrow neat. Not only will your own emotions begin to distract you; sooner or later, the rest of the world will likewise resume asserting its many needs. Well before you feel you are ready, you will have to go to work and clean the kitchen and pay the phone bill; you will have to listen to other people talking about the Nats game or the Congressional Black Caucus or daylight saving time; you will get mad about something unrelated, and laugh about something unrelated, and look at your partner and think about nothing at all except taking off her clothes. And the same goes for happiness. Nobody ever says "life goes on" after someone falls in love, but it does. As wonderful as those early besotted days are, you will not get to spend forever gazing into your beloved's eyes and making middle-of-the-night pancakes and staying in bed together until two in the afternoon. Eventually, some new development will command your attention, and then some new development again after that.

This is the other idea implicit in "and": that something else is about to happen. When the word first appeared in the English language, it meant "next," and it still retains that tacit orientation toward the future. "X, Y, Z, and": appended to the end of anything, it is an anti–stop sign, an indication that we are not yet done. ("And?" we say to someone when they have fallen silent without finishing their story or making their point; by which we mean "keep going.") As a result, the feeling of "and" is not just a feeling of conjunction; it is also a feeling of continuation. The abundance toward which it gestures—the sense that there is always something more—is not only spatial but also temporal.

This abundance is one of the most wonderful things about life, and also one of the most difficult, because it throws into relief the constraints of our own existence. The world overflows with possibilities—with places to visit and things to learn and books to read and skills to master and people to meet and causes to champion and trajectories to pursue—but only a tiny fraction of them are available to each of us. As a result, although we all like to feel that we make choices about our life, much of what we do amounts to choosing *against* things, to making our peace with everything that we will never get to do. From the age of six or seven until my early twenties, for instance, I entertained the idea of pursuing many different careers: a wizard, a squire, a gymnast, a jockey, a novelist, a historian, an astronaut, a mathematician, a mountaineer.

I love my life and wouldn't exchange it for any other, but I am not sure the faint contrails of longing left behind by all these other imagined futures ever fully disappear. That's not because some part of me still wonders who else I could have been; it is just a general mourning for the foreclosure of possibility. So many opportunities are out of reach from the moment we are born, ruled out by circumstance, and so many more are eliminated as we age. "It is impossible to have every experience," Virginia Woolf wrote, regretfully; at best we get a glimpse of a sliver of what we are missing— "like those glances I cast into basements when I walk in London streets." Decades later, the poet Louise Glück described this problem as "metaphysical claustrophobia: the bleak fate of being always one person." Every other possible existence, in Idaho or Honduras or Lahore, as a carpenter or baseball player or musical genius, as a sibling if we are an only child or an only child if we are the youngest of seven— all of these variations on the human experience are unavailable to us. We have, unavoidably, only our one lifetime, and no matter how energetic or interested or fortunate or long-lived we may be, we can only do so much with it. And so much, against the backdrop of the universe, can seem so very little.

That is the essential difficulty of our situation: life goes on, but we do not. We stop. Perhaps the devout are right and some part of us will endure beyond the grave, but either way, existence as we know it—falling in love, grieving, going to the grocery store, splashing in the ocean, driving at night with the music up and the windows down, in every detail good and difficult living out our days here among the egrets and herons and black bears and fleas: all of this ceases absolutely upon our death. That is the very essence of what it means to be mortal, yet it is difficult to fully imagine, let alone accept. Our lives are literally everything to us, and they feel so brimming and momentous while we are living them that it is hard to grasp how fleeting they are compared to the whole of human history, to say nothing of the vast sweep of space and time.

This radical discrepancy between the scale of our own lives and the scale of the rest of existence can leave us feeling two different ways. One of them, akin to the feeling of losing something, is that the universe is dauntingly large and we are terrifyingly insignificant. The other, akin to the feeling of finding, is that the universe is dauntingly large and yet here we are, unimaginably unlikely and therefore precious beyond measure. As with so many other contrasting feelings, most of us will experience both of these eventually. It is easy to feel small and powerless; easy, too, to feel amazed and fortunate to be here.

On the whole, though, I take the side of amazement. I cannot look closely for any length of time at even so simple a thing as a pond and do otherwise. This is what I realized that day at the arboretum: that what serves us best, in the face of inexorable loss, is not our grief or our acquiescence but our attention. For now, at least, the world is ours to notice and to change, and that seems to me sufficient. It is true that loss will ultimately part us from it, but it is also true, as I said earlier, that we have many bindings. Our works of art, our honorable deeds, our acts of kindness and generosity: all of these link us in unseen ways to future generations. So, too, does having children, that ultimate act of conjunction and continuation. Once, when I was nine or ten, I overheard my father joking that having kids didn't keep you young, but if you were lucky, it made you a little bit eternal. I understand now what he was saying, and I feel the meaning of both his life and my own stretching outward beyond our days, because C. and I are expecting a baby.

For me, the approach of parenthood has made obvious what is true for all of us, whether or not we ever have children: that we are here above all as caretakers, a role as essential as it is temporary. None of us would be here without what came before us, and none of us can know how much and in what ways everything that will come after us depends upon our being here. Walt Whitman, who understood the world's abundance as well as anyone who ever lived, understood this, too. Leaning on the railing of that Brooklyn ferry, dazzled by the view, he traveled over the waters and the centuries, then looked back and saw himself inseparably connected to everyone else who had undertaken that same journey. Life may exceed us, he knew, but for now it is also made of us. We are the "and," a part of the continuation of things, the binding between the present and the future.

That is all we have, this moment with the world. It will not last, because nothing lasts. Entropy, mortality, extinction: the entire plan of the universe consists of losing, and no matter how much we find along the way, life amounts to a reverse savings account in which we are eventually robbed of everything. Our dreams and plans and jobs and knees and backs and memories; the keys to the house, the keys to the car, the keys to the kingdom, the kingdom itself: sooner or later, all of it drifts into the Valley of Lost Things.

And so I know that what I have with C. is temporary. Someday I will lose her as I lost my father; or I will lose her as my father lost me, swept away at the close of life along with everything. One and then the other of us will die. We will grieve and be mourned and then be mourned no longer; our future child's grandchildren will scarcely know our names. A hundred years from now, the little spot where we got married will be gone, too—lost, together with much of the rest of the Eastern Shore, to a rising ocean. Whole species that live here will eventually disappear as well, gone the way of the dawn horse, gone the way of the megalodon. Time, in carrying on, will carry almost all of what we know of life away.

Nothing about that is strange or surprising; it is the fundamental, unalterable nature of things. The astonishment is all in the being here. It is the turtle in the pond, the thought in the mind, the falling star, the stranger on Main Street. It is the sunlit green I saw in C.'s eyes again first thing this morning, and the happiness I will feel in an hour or two when I end another day in her arms. To all of this, loss, which seems only to take away, adds its own kind of necessary contribution. No matter what goes missing, the object you need or the person you love, the lessons are always the same. Disappearance reminds us to notice, transience to cherish, fragility to defend. Loss is a kind of external conscience, urging us to make better use of our finite days. Our crossing is a brief one, best spent bearing witness to all that we see: honoring what we find noble, tending what we know needs our care, recognizing that we are inseparably connected to all of it, including what is not yet upon us, including what is already gone. We are here to keep watch, not to keep.

ACKNOWLEDGMENTS

I once heard the late Anthony Bourdain say of my agent, Kimberly Witherspoon, that if she called him up at three in the morning and told him to grab some duct tape, a knife, and a roll of garbage bags and meet her in fifteen minutes on the corner of Ninth Street and Avenue C, he'd be there on time, no questions asked. I could not hope to improve on that description of the trust and loyalty that Kim inspires in people, chiefly by being so loyal and trustworthy herself. She is the finest possible custodian of my career, not to mention wickedly fun, and I am extraordinarily lucky to call her both my agent and my friend. I'm also grateful to all of the other wonderful and helpful people at Inkwell Management, especially Alexis Hurley.

I think I actually *have* met Hilary Redmon on a street corner in Manhattan in the small hours of the night, because long before she became the editor of this book, she became my friend. It was a great comfort to me, especially during the more difficult moments of working on "Lost," to know that I could count on her not just for astute editing but for consummate humanity and kindness. She has been an indefatigable champion of this book from the beginning, and I cannot express enough gratitude to her and to all of her colleagues at Random House, including Carrie Neill, Ayelet Durantt, and Ruth Liebmann, whose enthusiasm arrived in my inbox exactly when I needed it.

My editor at *The New Yorker*, Henry Finder, does not pronounce his surname like "one who finds," but he nonetheless found me, and I will never stop being grateful. Here as everywhere, my writing benefited tremendously from his generosity, and from the range and perspicacity of his mind. Together with David Remnick—editor extraordinaire and mensch nonpareil—he has given me the best and happiest professional home I could ever hope to have. I am indescribably thankful to them both for their time and their faith, as well as for making room in the magazine for the essay that was the genesis of this book.

I would also like to thank other friends and colleagues who took the time to read this book and make it better: Jared Hohlt, for being my editor even when he is no longer my editor; Tad Friend, for an unexpected and extremely fun manuscript swap and the resulting clear-eyed read; Jia Tolentino, for her unstinting enthusiasm and incisiveness; Leslie Jamison, for one of the most wonderful editorial notes ever written, and for holding up the highway sign that said NARRATIVE; Helen Macdonald, for understanding as well as anyone the challenges of writing about grief and for knowing where to begin, plus everything else; and Michael Kavanagh, for the immensely patient and helpful readings and rereadings of this and all things, and for the companionship in laughter and grief. Many thanks also to Becca Laurie, for being the best P.I. and the best design eye in the business, and to Ben Phelan for the thoroughgoing fact-checking. All remaining errors are strictly my own, especially any pertaining to Ogden Nash.

This book is largely about family, and I could not have written it if my own, both given and chosen, were not so unfailingly loving and supportive. I can never sufficiently thank Bill and Sandy Cep, who trusted me first with their daughter and then with their story. Anyone who knows them also knows what an honor it is to be treated like one of their own. Similarly, Katelin Cep and Melinda Cep welcomed me into their lives from the beginning with open arms, not to mention matching pajamas, road trips, and the ultimate sacrifice of half-chocolate birthday cake.

I do not doubt that it is a mixed blessing to have a writer in the family, and perhaps especially so during times of grief, yet my mother, Margot Schulz, and my sister, Laura Schulz, never for a moment wavered in their support of me and of this book. Because the story I tell in its opening section is, for obvious reasons, chiefly about my father, my mother gets credit there only for teaching me good grammar and good manners. In reality, she also taught me patience, attentiveness, generosity, forbearance, and kindness, all through unflagging example. My sister, that scatterbrain, in fact has one of the finest minds as well as one of the finest hearts I've ever known; I see in her not only the best of my father but also the best of this world. She keeps me honest and makes me laugh, and has brought me, along with countless other joys, the joy of growing close to her own family: Sue Kaufman, Rachel Novick, MJ Kaufman, Henry Philofsky, and Adele Kaufman-Schulz—and, through them, to Steve Novick, Aviva Stahl, and Sabrina Bremer. All of them are very dear to me, and central to my life in ways not always visible in these pages.

Not all of this book was easy to write, but one large swath of it was: the love story that forms the heart of

"Found" and continues through "And." When I was working on those sections, I wrote each day, then brought the draft pages up to bed each night to read them aloud to Casey Cep, who inspired them. It brought me great comfort and great happiness to share them with her, as it brings me great comfort and great happiness to share everything with her, and she has made them, together with the rest of the manuscript and the rest of my life, immeasurably better. This book is for her, in the profound hope that it is only the beginning of the story. And it is also for my father—in the words once more of Robert Frost, the tribute of the current to the source.

ABOUT THE AUTHOR

KATHRYN SCHULZ is a staff writer at *The New Yorker* and the author of *Being Wrong.* She won a National Magazine Award and a Pulitzer Prize in 2015 for "The Really Big One," an article about seismic risk in the Pacific Northwest. *Lost & Found* grew out of "Losing Streak," which was originally published in *The New Yorker* and later anthologized in *The Best American Essays.* Her other essays and reporting have appeared in *The Best American Science and Nature Writing, The Best American Travel Writing,* and *The Best American Food Writing.* A native of Ohio, she lives with her family on the Eastern Shore of Maryland.

kathrynschulz.com

WITHDRAWN

1/2022
$27.00